A Kinder Shift to Wellness

5 Paths *to a* Low-Stress, Elevated Life

JAN KINDER, RN

HYGIEIA PRESS

The information contained in this book is providing general and anecdotal information for educational purposes and is not intended to be a substitute for professional medical advice, diagnosis, opinion, treatment, or service. Any medical advice quoted by the author in this book is paraphrased and/or quoted and should not reflect on the actual advice given by your personal health care provider. Consult with your personal health care provider first before starting any new practices or health programs.

Published by
Hygieia Press
DELRAY BEACH, FL
www.jankinder.com

Copyright © 2021 Jan Kinder

ISBN-13: 978-0-5787781-4-3

All rights reserved. This book or any portion thereof may not be reproduced, or used in any manner whatsoever without the express written permission of the publisher except for personal practices. You may record only the guided imagery scripts for your personal or private use. You may not make recordings or reproduce anything else from this book.

Edited by Carol Killman Rosenberg

Cover and interior design by Gary A. Rosenberg

Author photo by Suzanne Barton Photography

To my loving mother, Jean Siudmak.
Thank you for the gift of life,
for your unconditional love,
for believing in me, and
for encouraging me to trust in my dreams
and to envision what can be.

Contents

Foreword by Brian Luke Seaward, PhD...................vii

Preface: My Journey...xi

Introduction..1

Part One: Awakening Change for Growth

Chapter 1: Turning Points Transform Your Life......... 9

Chapter 2: Five Lessons to Be Learned.................15

Chapter 3: Stress as an Opportunity for Growth 25

Chapter 4: Embracing the Concept of Change..........35

Part Two: Free the Mind, Access Your Inner Wisdom

Chapter 5: Accessing the Higher Self Is Key.............49

Chapter 6: Finding Joy in the Stillness....................58

Chapter 7: Discovering Who You Are.....................70

Chapter 8: The Power of Intention........................76

Part Three: Daily Rituals for a Healthier You

Chapter 9: Aligning Your Biological Rhythms..........87

Chapter 10: Letting Go of the Day...................... 100

Chapter 11: Coping Strategies 110

Chapter 12: Your Personal Relaxation Plan 120

Part Four: Emotional Healing, Meaningful Relationships

Chapter 13: The Positive Side of Anger 135

Chapter 14: Releasing Fear-Based Beliefs 145

Chapter 15: The Art of Relationships 154

Part Five: Elevate and Align Your Energy

Chapter 16: What's Energy Got to Do with It? 167

Chapter 17: Healing Through the Chakras 181

Chapter 18: Energy Management 197

Chapter 19: Healing Mysteries of Sound and Music: Part I 209

Chapter 20: Healing Mysteries of Sound and Music: Part II 222

My Parting Words 239

Recommended Reading to Inspire 241

References 243

Acknowledgments 246

About the Author 249

Foreword

I first heard the word "wellness" spoken with great aplomb by Dr. Elizabeth Kübler-Ross in 1981. She was the keynote speaker at the second annual American Holistic Medical Association Conference in La Crosse, Wisconsin. Renowned for her work on the topic of death and dying, her keynote didn't address this wisdom that spring day. Rather, her presentation was on the topic of holistic wellness. "Wellness," she said, "is a word new to the American vernacular, but the concept is ageless. It goes back thousands and thousands of years." She went on to say that "wellness" is best defined as integration, balance, and harmony of mind, body, spirit, and emotions, where the whole is always greater than the sum of the parts. As she said this, she drew a big circle on a flip chart. "There is much wisdom expressed in the symbol of a circle," she said.

So much more than the absence of disease, wellness conveys a sense of wholeness, as expressed through the timeless symbol of a circle. Examples of wholeness are abundant throughout all the cultures around the planet, from the full moon and peace symbol to the dinner plate and Christmas wreath, to name a few. Many corporate logos are created in the shape of a circle to convey a sense of wholeness. Wisdom keepers throughout the ages have depicted the holistic aspects of wellness through stories (e.g., the Hero's Journey) and artwork (e.g., the Taoist yin/yang symbol, the Tibetan mandala, and the sacred hoop of the American Indian culture). And . . . should you ever forget your inherent wholeness, all you need do is look in the mirror and see not one but two circles in the beauty of wholeness in your eyes. There is much wisdom expressed in the symbol of a circle!

Since I first heard the word "wellness" used in the context of holism, I have taken a great affinity toward all things wellness. I am not alone. Over the past several decades, the concepts of wellness have been embraced by nearly all allied health professionals and, particularly, the public at large. Despite a hunger for a richer state of health, the vast majority of people still see wellness as merely physical well-being, or what I refer to with my tongue in my cheek, as "broccoli and aerobics," now "Kale and CrossFit." What I learned long ago and had validated by mentors and wisdom keepers like Elizabeth Kübler-Ross is that wellness is so much more than the absence of disease, so much more than physical health. Let's take a closer look at each of the four major components, where the whole is always greater than the sum of the parts:

Physical well-being: the optimal functioning of all the body's physiological systems (e.g., cardiovascular, immune, endocrine, etc.).

Mental well-being: the ability to gather, process, recall, and communicate information.

Emotional well-being: the ability to feel and express the entire range of human emotions (from anger to love) and to control them, not be controlled by them.

Spiritual well-being: A sense of higher consciousness as expressed through the aspects of one's relationships (internal and external), values, and a meaningful purpose in one's life.

Physical wellness (broccoli and aerobics) gets the lion's share of the attention because it is so quantifiable. Heart rate, blood pressure, cholesterol, and even one's DNA history can be measured. But if this is all we focus on, then we enter a state of dysfunction. By denying the essential aspects of the other three components, we deny ourselves the fulfillment of our highest potential.

The world has become a very stressed planet these days. Incivility, climate change, economic downturns, digital toxicity, alienation, and isolation are but a few of the serious problems humanity faces at the dawn of the twenty-first century. Yet stress has always been part of the human landscape. Where there is chronic stress, there is the opportunity for a compromise in one's health and wellness. Over the past several decades we have learned that while people have succumbed to the pressures of stress, others have thrived. What this reveals is that we can all thrive in the face of stress, if we choose to take a different path.

Picture this: You are on a hike with many miles yet to complete your sojourn, and you are thirsty. Your water bottle is nearly empty, just a drop or two left. Up ahead in the distance is another person, and you smile with a sigh of relief. As you approach, you see this woman sitting at an ancient well. She kindly offers you a drink, and you accept gladly. This book you are holding in your hands is more than a collection of words, stories, and wisdom. It is a cup of wisdom drawn from the waters of this well. Jan is more than the book's author; she is the woman at the well offering you a drink and a means to fill your cup. Jan understands the integration, balance, and harmony of mind, body, spirit, and emotions. Moreover, she understands the nature of stress and both the subtle and dynamic means to cope with stress successfully. She has cleverly integrated this wisdom into what she calls the five paths to a low-stress, elevated life.

To no surprise, the well Jan stands at is a circle. It's a spring that gathers to share its healing waters that collect well below the earth's surface, so that all who pass may benefit. The five paths Jan outlines and illustrates are the cornerstones to the well of life. Take a moment to sit at the well before you drink. Sip this wisdom slowly and let it hydrate your human spirit. Fill your water bottle for the next leg of your journey, and remember, you can and should return to this well often.

Brian Luke Seaward, PhD
Author, *Stand Like Mountain, Flow Like Water*
Boulder, CO
www.brianlukeseaward.net

PREFACE

My Journey

My journey began by being born into a medical and musical family. My father, a surgeon and accomplished pianist, favored discipline and learning classical piano, which I began at age five. Later on, I grew to appreciate his incredible gift of music. He also believed in the principles of what we today call "alternative medicine." My mother was a nurse, a pianist, and a visionary. Unconditional love was her number-one core value. She was a gifted healer with a strong spiritual practice and encouraged my spiritual exploration early on. My aunt, a practicing Buddhist from Thailand, taught me how to meditate when I was a child. I didn't realize at the time just how strongly my formative years would guide and define my destiny.

At thirteen, I encountered the first turning point in my life. I was diagnosed with osteochondritis dissecans of the knee, a joint disorder. After surgery, I was instructed to wear a knee brace and avoid weight-bearing sports. Instead of letting my experience limit me, I started testing my limits. I took on gymnastics and cheerleading, and pored over the only book on hatha yoga I could find at the public library and started to play with yoga postures and the breath. My inquisitive nature came out as I experimented with different ways of breathing, using different types of music to affect my emotions, and meditating on a candle flame. I knew deep down, even back then, that I could change how I felt inside and out. I believed it was possible to heal myself.

I pursued a career in nursing, wanting to combine medicine, music, and ancient practices to help people heal. In my last year of nursing school, I met Dr. Elisabeth Kübler-Ross, who was serving as a guest lecturer discussing the five stages of grief in her groundbreaking book *On Death and Dying*. She shared her work in art therapy with the terminally ill, and, knowing I was a pianist, she encouraged me to include music therapy in my work. She planted a seed in me.

Having completed my nursing training and bachelor's degree in psychology, I soon realized that my use of meditation, breathing, and music therapy practices placed me ahead of my time in the medical world of the 1970s. Despite my patients' reduced suffering, stress, and pain, I did not receive much support from many of my colleagues for my way of thinking. Resources on alternative approaches within the medical community were few and far between at the time. I knew I needed to go on my own learning quest to evolve spiritually, personally, and professionally. I was to become an advocate for wellness and a pioneer in holistic nursing and the healing arts.

At that juncture, I had two major turning points: First, I was blessed to marry my best friend, a brilliant, creative, and spiritual man. Then I was told I had an autoimmune disease. After a month of prescription, high-dose steroids and their unpleasant side effects, I decided it was time for a radical change. I completely shifted my approach and chose an alternative medicine path. For the next eight months and under the direction and care of a remarkable healer, Talib Schwartz, I followed a concentrated plan of acupuncture, shiatsu, qigong, and Chinese herbs. I also combined meditation, visualizations, and music to relax and help with the pain and inflammation. I was determined to get well. Two years later, there were no signs of the illness. I realized how I had been thinking and working to shift the energy inside me had led to my healing. My healing started with *me*.

Following my positive experience, I pursued formal studies with master teachers in these alternative practices—another major turning point. I left hospital nursing to seek avenues to combine Western medicine with alternative and Eastern medicine, music in medicine, and spirituality. This included music therapy, just as Dr. Kübler-Ross had suggested. I became a certified music therapist using Carl Orff's model for music and movement pedagogy with emphasis on child development.

Over the next decade, I committed myself to professional growth and spiritual studies. I immersed myself in the healing arts, mind-body interventions, and energy therapies. I learned relaxation techniques, guided imagery, music and sound therapy, spiritual healing, yoga, and qigong. My initial mission to help people cope with stress and illness and enhance their quality of life continues to be my mission four decades later. To feed my soul, I learned about Jain meditation and the path to self-realization through the human energy system (chakras), sound, and color with Gurudev Shree Chitrabhanuji. Later, my meditation practice shifted to Nichiren Shoshu Buddhism and chanting the lotus sutra, *Nam Myoho Renge Kyo*, a practice to receive compassion and wisdom for enlightenment.

From 1979 to 1989, I founded and ran the healing arts and music therapy programs for adults and children at Turtle Bay Music School (TBMS) in New York City, with outreach programs to four local schools. I sought to support a multisensory approach in self-expression through music and the arts to foster self-esteem and personal development. The Young People's Division I created grew from 11 to 300 families.

In 1981, I established the music therapy/music in medicine programs at Rusk Institute for Rehabilitation Medicine (RIRM) at NYU. My nursing background helped me bring music and the healing arts into mainstream medicine. This was a milestone back then.

In 1984, Ruth "Sis" Frank, an innovative woman in St. John in the US Virgin Islands, reached out to me. She wanted to create an arts education school there to include the programs I was conducting in NYC. I traveled to St. John frequently to discuss plans and later led a few introductory workshops. I fell in love with St. John and the people there.

These ten years were full of learning, joy, and fulfilling my visions and dreams. Then came another major turning point: I was ready to welcome a new mission, an exciting adventure.

In 1989, I appointed my successors at TBMS and RIRM. While maintaining residence in the States, my husband and I moved to St. John so I could help develop and teach programs at the St. John School of the Arts (SJSA). With much enthusiasm and vision, I conducted classes and workshops for children and adults in music therapy and expressive movement, wellness and the healing arts, meditation, and other community interests for women. I also maintained a private practice in music therapy and stress management.

Over the next five years, I had fun, but I took on a lot of responsibility, working around the clock. My spiritual and daily practices slowly disappeared; there were not enough hours in a day and I lacked energy. I didn't know I was stressed out. I consumed a lot of carbs and sugar to keep going. My energy was high, but I was exhausted. I was overwhelmed and the body knew it. Yet my mind was clueless.

Then in 1994, I got my wake-up call. On the eve of my fortieth birthday, I had a near-death experience. I had a ruptured ectopic pregnancy. My breathing practices and meditation helped control the pain, but I hemorrhaged for twenty-two hours before surgery could be performed on another island and there was no available blood to transfuse me. My recovery was dependent on *me*. While this may sound odd to you, this episode was the best thing that ever happened to me; it changed me on every level. It took a near-death for me to finally learn.

Over the next three months, I had time to contemplate my near-death experience, to heal, and to dive deep into my wellness practices. I came to some realizations: my love for my work had blinded me to how the pressure and stress I was under had truly affected me. I got caught up in the energy of doing, and my ego took control and overshadowed all of my previous practices. I would tell people, "I know how to relax," and "I know how to deal with stress," and "I'm fine." But when I was laid up in bed, I had no choice but to listen to what the body and my soul needed. I realized that healing needed to be on a more profound level. It was imperative that I ask the necessary questions to uncover the root cause and discover not only the physical but also the emotional and spiritual issues surrounding my experience. I needed to open my awareness and wake up to a new way of thinking.

On the advice of my friend Diane Kennedy, I attended a weeklong healing seminar with Dr. Deepak Chopra and Dr. David Simon. I immediately knew I was in the right place with the right teachers for me. This was to be another major turning point. I began in-depth studies with them and with Roger Gabriel, which included a lot of self-inquiry, self-awareness, and lifestyle practices. I learned about the ancient alternative health system known as Ayurveda and mantra meditation. When the Chopra Center opened in 1996, I was thrilled to be among the first Chopra Center certified instructors teaching Ayurveda and Primordial Sound (Mantra) Meditation.

In 1996, I founded the Mind Body Health Institute and divided my time between St. John and the States, teaching the Chopra Center programs and speaking to various organizations. As a holistic nurse, I developed a private practice in stress management. When my clients and students in the States asked that I bring them on a retreat with me to St. John, I listened to my inner spirit and decided to create a center at Caneel Bay Resort, a special place with no phones or televisions in the rooms, a perfect setting for what I was guided to manifest.

To that end, I founded The Self Centre International at Caneel Bay Resort in St. John, USVI, in January 2000, which quickly became an internationally recognized and award-winning mind-body-spirit wellness center. I knew I aligned with a greater divine purpose because creating the center was effortless. The energy surrounding the concept attracted staff, clients, and the media. Along with my team of instructors and therapists, we offered an array of approaches, such as yoga, tai chi, meditation, couple's classes, sacred feminine circles, chakra balancing, vibrational sound and color therapies, shamanism, and energy healing.

The philosophy was to create a one-of-a-kind experience leading to a personal transformation. The Self Centre was recognized by the media as an innovative leader in the hotel wellness industry.

That same year, I broadened my knowledge of sound therapy, which was another major turning point. I had the opportunity to study and become a practitioner with Tama-Do: the Academy of Sound, Color and Movement® with the renowned Fabien Maman, father of vibrational sound therapy, and Faery Shaman Terres Unsoeld. Tama-Do ("Way of the Soul") opened me to a deeper understanding of my existence. The science and art of sound and color therapy Fabien and Terres taught was unsurpassed.

Throughout this time, my alliance with St. John School of the Arts remained strong. In addition to The Self Centre, I offered my services at the school as a faculty member and assistant director. I also introducced the Mind Body Connection for Scholastic Improvement in-school program, teaching yoga, meditation, and relaxation techniques to the children. Later on I was appointed executive director of SJSA (2006–2011), and to this day, I am still on the advisory council.

The last major turning point came with the passing of my mother in 2009 and of Sis Frank ten months later. My mother's sudden departure turned my world upside down. She had been my best friend and rock. I would need to develop a new sense of courage and strength in her absence. Sis's passing was also emotionally hard; I had taken care of her, like a daughter, in the last years of her amazing life. I began to see my life's purpose differently. Intuitively, I knew the energy had changed, for I had shifted. I received the clear message to move back to the States, but I had no definitive plan other than to completely trust. Within the year, it became clear I was exactly where I needed to be. Everything was in perfect order.

Two years prior, I decided to reconnect with my nursing roots through the American Holistic Nurses Association (AHNA) and become board-certified in holistic nursing and board-certified in health and wellness nurse coaching. I'm glad I did. The nurse coaching was an added plus for my clients. I was also drawn to Brian Luke Seaward, PhD, the leading international authority in holistic stress management. His approach, teaching, and guidance helped me pull together decades of my work in stress management. In addition, I incorporated the work of Julianne Bien, combining Lumalight color light therapy with geometrical shapes into my services.

I now live in beautiful South Florida, still married to my best friend, offering my services with my precious Shih Tzu and sidekick healing dog, Asia, and speaking. Mind-body-spirit interrelatedness and enhancing the quality of life remain the themes of my personal and professional life. I have been truly blessed and know that my life is guided by unconditional love and divine intervention. For this, I am eternally grateful.

I bring all the experiences I had on this journey to this book to share with you some of the knowledge, experience, and insight I've gained over this lifetime. The principles and practices have helped me shift my perceptions, change my choices, and guide me toward expressing my soul's inner light so I may live my true essence. Perhaps they will shed a new light for you, too.

Introduction

Every human being basically wants the same things: to live a joyful, healthy, and harmonious life. Everyone desires to feel a sense of wellness, to feel whole. Wellness is a holistic and complex phenomenon that considers all aspects of well-being. Health is viewed as the dynamic and equal integration of our eight dimensions of wellness: physical, mental, emotional, spiritual, social, occupational, environmental, and financial. The National Wellness Institute defines wellness as "a conscious, self-directed and evolving process of achieving full potential." Wellness is a process of change and growth through healthy and positive lifestyle habits and choices. Well-being is the state of optimal health and happiness that is experienced when balance and wellness is attained.

Stress is, nevertheless, commonplace in our society; we are living in a world of rapid change, constant pressure, and uncertainty. Our schedules are so full, we have limited time to stop, relax, and regroup. What gets sacrificed? Our happiness. Our health. Our sense of peace. Our sense of self. What matters most to us in life gets disrupted. Stress and an overpacked schedule may be causing you to sacrifice your need to

❖ Stay healthy, so you can enjoy life now and as you get older.

❖ Get a good night's sleep, so you can get up in the morning feeling refreshed.

❖ Spend quality time with family and friends doing what you love to do without the guilt.

- Feel a sense of connection to something bigger than yourself.
- Feel energized and motivated to express your creativity in all that you do.
- Be aware and appreciate all that life has to offer.
- Have fun and enjoy the life you want to create and that you deserve.

Unmanaged long-term stress affects every system in the body and may lead to a myriad of debilitating illnesses or can worsen existing disease conditions. It has been noted that 80 to 90 percent of all chronic diseases are stress-related and therefore preventable.

Do you always know when you are under stress? Or are you, like I once was, constantly on the go, with the pressures of having to get things done while at the same time having a great time, clueless about your stress level? The fun I was experiencing was masking the obvious signs of stress the body was undergoing. The body shouted, but I couldn't, or should I say wouldn't, hear. I was in a zone. The effects of stress were present, but I was unaware. I was distracted.

The Wellness Path

What does wellness mean to you? Take a moment to reflect on what it means to be well. Notice what comes to mind. When you choose a path toward wellness, do you consider balancing all aspects of your life?

Reducing the accumulated effects of stress, nurturing the body, and introducing ways to interrupt the stress response are vital. Learning ways to adapt to and cope with anger, anxiety, and fear while releasing emotional toxicity is needed. Relaxation techniques are essential in creating a quality life. Turning our attention toward our spiritual nature allows our inner wisdom, our inner soul, to be our greatest creative resource.

The information and practices I share in this book break down how to create wellness in your life into easy-to-follow steps. It's the small, practical steps that make the most profound changes that stick. You will receive practices, skills, tools, and strategies to move forward and grow. Be patient and kind with yourself throughout this process of transformation. As it has been said, "Rome was not built in a day." Know that it takes thirty days to introduce a new habit in your life and ninety days to make it a part of your everyday lifestyle.

Healing and wellness are an ongoing process. My healing didn't happen overnight. Over the years, I've invested time, money, and energy to make the necessary changes to shift from the inside out to create health and well-being in my life. The decisions I made every step of the way were not always easy, but I persevered. I had my practices in the healing arts to help support my vision of how I wanted my life to be. I would recall my near-death experience, which I shared a bit about in the preface, and remind myself to not let that happen again. I made a vow to myself to commit 100 percent of myself to my physical, mental, emotional, and spiritual wellness. I encourage you to make a commitment to yourself. There is a direct correlation between your level of commitment and your success in achieving your goals and vision. Become your own best friend.

How to Use This Book

This book is a holistic approach to stress management. *Holistic* means to look at balancing the whole person to create physical, mental, emotional, and spiritual health and overall well-being. There are a multitude of ways to balance and heal. Throughout this book, you will discover how to free the mind and tap into your inner wisdom, enjoy nourishing self-care wellness practices, cope with stress, learn to develop healthy loving relationships with yourself and others, and elevate your energy for a more harmonious and resilient life. As you apply what you learn, you will begin to feel the effects of change. You can start to feel calm and relaxed, more in balance, and in control. You will shift from living on automatic pilot to being more aware and mindful of what you are thinking, doing, and feeling. You can love and appreciate yourself with a boost of self-confidence. *A Kinder Shift to Wellness* teaches you how to create the change necessary to shift your lifestyle behaviors and practices to support wellness.

As a result of your participation in the practices and self-inquiry exercises shared in this book, you will

- Rediscover the body's own inner intelligence for emotional freedom.
- Integrate simple, proven habits that support vibrant health and well-being.
- Learn how to clear stress with more ease.
- Explore ways to let go and deeply relax.
- Discover what it takes for a healthy relationship with yourself and others.
- Optimize your inner and outer energy to bring more harmony and happiness into your life.

> I recommend getting two journals and a set of colored pencils. The first journal gives you space to respond to the questions and prompts in this book. The second journal is for an insightful bedtime practice you will learn in Chapter 10. The colored pencils are for certain self-inquiry exercises.

A Kinder Shift to Wellness incorporates the practices I've used successfully with my clients over the years. This book is divided into five parts. Each part begins with the learning goals for the chapters in that part. Each chapter opens with a discussion and then offers practices and takeaways. You will read stories of client experiences to help you better understand the information presented. Inside the chapters are self-inquiry exercises and then a review of the key points to close. There is a recommended reading and resource section at the end.

One chapter builds upon the next, so read the chapters in order. You may either read the book straight through, and then go back and do the practices and exercises, or you can go through each chapter and participate along the way. It's your choice. If you consistently need more time—greater than two or three weeks—to complete a chapter, you may want to ask yourself what is holding you back. Are you experiencing resistance? Did a personal or family issue arise that required your attention? Are you procrastinating? Has a work commitment created a distraction? Are you having other challenges? Be aware of the situation, adjust where you can, and reevaluate your level of commitment to yourself. It's all okay. It's all a part of the learning sequence. Change is a process of self-awareness. Whatever you decide, know that change is a personal decision.

I hope you find this book helpful and inspiring. Reading this book and doing the practices and exercises is like having me as your personal coach guiding you every step of the way. And if this book turns out to be just a fascinating read, then that's alright, too. I wish you well on your journey of self-care and self-discovery.

If you want to know how you can work with me, you are welcome to visit www.JanKinder.com.

PART ONE

Awakening Change for Growth

"Awakening is not changing who you are but discarding who you are not."
—DEEPAK CHOPRA

Are you ready to turn a page in your life? Do you want to start a new chapter and create a new adventure to support a life free of chaos and overwhelming stress? Are you ready to make wellness, resilience, happiness, and peace a way of life? If you want to make that shift starting today, I welcome you.

You and I will be walking the path of transformation to reclaim your life. You will become clear on where change is needed, acknowledge your stressors, and recognize the potential for growth. After completing the practices and self-inquiries in this part, you will be able to

❖ Recognize your wake-up call, the turning point awakening you to change.

❖ Acknowledge what traits are needed in your life for transformation to occur.

- Explore the stressors, obstacles, and distractions in your life.
- Understand how stress can be an opportunity for personal and spiritual growth.

My commitment to you is to give you what you need to begin your journey on solid ground. I will give you the specific, proven skills and strategies for you to succeed. You may be looking to sleep better and have more energy. You may be searching for peace and happiness, for a life without the chaos, drama, and stress. Maybe you are looking to build your resilience to face life's challenges with more ease. Whatever your reason, it's no accident you are reading these words. I ask that you have faith in the process and faith in yourself. Stay focused and keep moving forward.

CHAPTER 1

Turning Points Transform Your Life

"You cannot change your destination overnight, but you can change your direction overnight."
—JIM ROHN

As you read in the Preface, several turning points influenced and changed the course of my life. For me, some of my major turning points involved physical issues, while others influenced my personal and spiritual growth. A few shifts were not the ideal path to follow and resulted in new choices. Many of my shifts were a welcome change filled with adventure and excitement. I used many of my turning points to redefine and reinvent myself. Are you aware of the turning points in your own life? Let's take a look.

Turning Points Are Catalysts for Change

As you go through life, you experience turning points that grab your attention and invite you to consider whether or not you should look at things differently. A turning point is a time when an important change happens. They are life's big lessons. Major turning points are catalysts for change and alter the course of your life's path. Change can be an opportunity. You are being presented with options, both consciously and unconsciously. Your inner self, your inner voice, is communicating with you. You are being asked to look at different choices, even when inner conflicts arise, and make a decision that helps promote a sense of wholeness and well-being in life. The turning points in your life, both subtle and profound, got you to where you are today.

Relationships with other people can be a turning point. These associations can greatly influence the course of someone's life. Family members, teachers, and mentors can be a source of inspiration for major change. Parents have reported how the birth of a child gave them a greater sense of purpose and a desire to create a good family life. Negative life situations involving family can turn into positive outcomes. John Walsh made the decision to turn the murder of his son, Adam, into a personal mission to help others. He became an anti-crime advocate and criminal investigator and created and hosted the TV show *America's Most Wanted*. Another example, a foster child, after experiencing repeated abuse, is finally placed in a loving home, and given the opportunity to experience happiness and live a productive life.

Keep in mind, not all turning points are major, life-altering events. Some stand out more than others while others are subtler. You may not even be aware when you have made a shift; it is not always obvious or visible. Consider times in your life when you experienced a change, perhaps when you graduated school, moved to a new city, or started a new job. Turning points can be external or internal. Maybe you had a shift in thinking or belief. Reading this book is a turning point. Whatever the catalyst for change, know that change is growth.

> *Keep in mind, not all turning points are major, life-altering events.*

There is no set of rules when it comes to your response and action with turning points. If you look back throughout your life, notice those points in time where everything shifted. Some turning points are positive while others can cause inner conflict. Turning points may not be easy to go through. Sometimes our choices were not the best choices at that time. Dwelling on those choices with regret goes nowhere. We recognize them, learn from them, and then move on, going forward with a new choice or direction. When you make the decision to change, it's not important to know the outcome beforehand. Allow the consequences to organically unfold.

Let's take a look at a few examples of some major turning points. A client of mine, Julie, a high-powered, unmarried corporate executive, got pregnant. She did not know how she was going to juggle her work, which involved traveling, and raising a child. Aborting or giving the child up for adoption was not an option. She wasn't keen on the idea of being in the background while a nanny raised her child. After a few coaching sessions with me, Julie realized motherhood was calling her, but she did not want to give up her autonomy. She found a way to have both. She chose to resign while she was still only two-and-a-half months pregnant. This would give her six months to develop and implement her plan. She decided to put her energy and contacts into creating an online business before the delivery of her baby. Julie chose to be a stay-at-home mom and raise her daughter, while working from home to build her business. She believes she has the best of both worlds and knows it was the best decision of her life.

I knew two sisters who had grown up with alcoholic parents. Their childhood was a nightmare, they said. They were exposed to their parents' shouting and witnessed the drunken stupor their parents fell into whenever they hosted a party, which was often. The sisters vowed to never be like their parents. Eventually, the sisters faced a turning point as they left home to start their lives. What choice would each make? Interestingly, each sister chose a different path, and they ended up with two very different lives. One followed in her parents' footsteps and became an alcoholic, spending time in and out of rehab. The other sister became a social worker and works in an alcohol and drug rehab facility. It's interesting that the factor that influenced both of their decisions was addiction.

As the story goes, Harrison Ford, a struggling actor, worked as a carpenter to make money and support his family. One day, he accepted a job to build cabinets in the home of George Lucas. While on the job, Lucas offered him a supporting role in his movie *American Graffiti*. Harrison auditioned and got the part. Later, Lucas would cast him in *Star Wars* as Han Solo. The rest is Hollywood history.

Mother Teresa, a Catholic nun, believed she received a calling from God. She described it as a "call within a call." This was the turning point that would change her life and the world forever. She went to Calcutta, India, and worked in the streets helping care for the very poor and sick. She made the decision to accept this turning point and her new, challenging, and selfless mission. Her work inspired nations, as she revealed the plight of suffering children and refugees. She later founded the worldwide order known as the Missionaries of Charity, an organization dedicated to unconditional love and helping the poor. In 1979, she was awarded the Nobel Peace Prize. In 2016, she was canonized as Saint Teresa of Calcutta. It's remarkable how one decision created such a change.

Some turning points are not as life altering or major as these previous examples, of course. For instance, a colleague of mine, after hearing about a family member diagnosed with Alzheimer's disease, now organizes fund-raising walks twice a year for Alzheimer's research. Her life is not noticeably different, but she has enriched it, as well as the lives of others. In another case, one of my clients was offered a new job. She chose not to accept the offer; her turning point was realizing that staying in her present position was the better decision. And here's one more: I have a friend who was very active on the dating scene, looking for a suitable life partner. Each man she dated was a turning point, resulting in subtle changes in her daily living habits and interests. Her life took many turns and she made many decisions until she settled down with her perfect match.

Once again, I encourage you to respond to the prompts and exercises in a journal. You can also use your journal for further self-inquiry and reflection. *I personally like to keep a journal so that I can look back and see my growth. A journal is a private, sacred place to share with yourself your deepest aspirations, thoughts, and desires.*

YOUR TURN FOR SELF-DISCOVERY

Congratulations for taking this first step. Turning points are incentives for growth. You know you need to make a change. How you live your life is your decision. Now, you have the power to make this moment in time a turning point in your life. I shared with you some of my turning points and the outcomes of those shifts. Now it's your turn.

Self-Inquiry Exercise: Before you begin, find a quiet place and allow 10 minutes for this exercise. Close the eyes and take a few deep breaths to focus your awareness. When you feel relaxed and centered, gently open the eyes. In your journal, respond to the following prompts with your thoughts and insights:

- ❖ What was the catalyst, your turning point, your wake-up call for change?

- ❖ What opened your awareness? What happened for you to say enough is enough?

- ❖ What would be the cost of inaction, staying where you are and not moving forward? How would it affect your overall well-being?

In Closing

Turning points can be significant events that literally change lives. They do not have to be major events. Some are subtler and sometimes you may not realize they're turning points until later. When it comes to your physical, mental, emotional, and spiritual wellness, it's valuable to know your turning points that brought you to where you are today. Here are a few points to remember from this chapter:

- Be aware of the times you experienced a major change and the decisions you made that created those changes.
- Recognize the potential for change when making decisions, especially when it comes to your health and well-being.
- Choosing wellness can be a major turning point.
- When you make the decision to change, it's not important to know the outcome.
- Acknowledge those who have inspired you to change and grow.
- Remember, some turning points are major events while others are smaller and can go unnoticed until later.

As you proceed to the next chapter, I will share the lessons I needed to learn after my near-death experience to start reclaiming my life.

CHAPTER 2

Five Lessons to Be Learned

"Transformation literally means going beyond your form."
—WAYNE DYER

It wasn't until my near-death experience that I had an awakening. I realized I had sacrificed my power. My encounter opened my eyes and heart and made me take a good look at every area of my life—physically, mentally, emotionally, and spiritually. It was my wake-up call. I could hear Spirit say to me, "How about I lay you up for three months so you can contemplate this?" During my physical recovery, the body became my teacher because it commanded my attention 24/7. The body forced me to look inward at myself. There was no escape.

My experience catapulted me into an in-depth look at myself that forced me to take full responsibility for my life. Realizing I had gotten off my path, like Dorothy in *The Wizard of Oz*, I knew I needed to raise my awareness and look inward for the answers. Change does not begin in the body. Change in our mindset begins in our consciousness. The body is the end result. What started as my three-month contemplation turned into a major transformation on every level of my being. I chose to heal the heart, change my beliefs, and connect with the light of Spirit to feel whole.

I will share with you the five lessons I needed to learn to start reclaiming my life and nurturing my soul: 1) Listen to the body, 2) Say yes to yourself, 3) Integrate, 4) Delegate, and 5) Elevate. Learning the value of living from the inside out, as opposed to the outside in, was paramount. Inside-out living allows us to tap into our inner wisdom to guide our thoughts, feelings, and behaviors. Wellness begins from within. You will be learning how to apply these five lessons throughout this book, but let's look at each now.

Listen to the Body

Does the body speak to you? Do you understand what it's saying? There are many lessons the body can teach, if we only know how to listen. It starts with being aware of how the body feels inside and out. Being present, being aware, is key. Right now, as you are reading these words, are you aware of how you are breathing? Simply notice the breath. Is the breath fast or slow? Deep or shallow? Are you breathing through the nose or mouth? Is the breath smooth or uneven? As you innocently observed the breath, what did you become aware of? Describe it to yourself.

It's important to sense and know how the body feels in the moment. Areas of discomfort are not to be ignored. These are signals that something is wrong. By listening to the body, you can remedy problems before they intensify.

Now check in with the entire body. Take a moment and scan from head to toe, and notice any areas of tension, sensations, or discomfort. If the body could speak, what would it be saying to you right now? Listen to its messages.

We want to listen when the body is whispering, "Help me." Waiting until the body shouts causes us to face a full-blown health predicament. This is what happened to me. I was so out of touch because of distractions that I wasn't paying attention to the body and didn't hear the whispers for help. If we tune in and listen, the body will communicate what it needs, whether it is food, exercise, rest, or medical attention.

Say Yes to Yourself

Do you find yourself saying yes to other people when you really want to say no? Before my health crisis occurred, I had fallen into an old trap of not honoring myself. It took five years for this fallback to happen. I was successful in and thrilled by what I was doing. However, as I helped to bring other people's visions to fruition, I lacked the autonomy and the ability to stand up for myself. I succumbed to working long hours, and my self-care practices suffered. I felt intimidated by authority figures, an old pattern of not questioning authority that I realized was still lingering from my childhood. Two childhood messages were that I was "not good enough" and that I "shouldn't be lazy." I was ready to take the necessary steps to make that change. I needed to remember to say yes to what I wanted for my life without guilt and kindly say no to others.

When I made the shift to saying yes to me again, my world opened to new opportunities. I set my vision and mission and created a mind-body-spirit wellness center in 1996. *Yes* and *no* are powerful words that have a great deal of energy behind them. Use them wisely.

Integrate

Do you wait until everything is in perfect order before you take the time to practice self-care? Do not wait until the end of the day, weekends, or vacation time to de-stress and relax.

The act of self-care, de-stressing, and relaxation is an ongoing process. Integrating practices throughout the day to keep yourself focused, nurtured, and balanced is essential for wellness. Coping with stressful situations as they are happening can help reduce the buildup of accumulated stress. Running around frantic, like a chicken without a head, to later indulge in moments of relaxation is not a balanced life. It's a roller coaster.

Years ago, I saw a comic strip that I will never forget. The first frame shows a woman rushing around at work. The next frame shows her stressed and frazzled trying to multitask. In the third frame, her hair is standing on end as she is speeding and driving her car recklessly. The final frame then shows her calmly sitting in a meditation position chanting "om." This cartoon was poking fun at the absurdity of rushing around frantically to then settle down in silence. It is ironic because a lot of people can relate. However, this type of lifestyle undermines the greater purpose of going through life balanced and calm.

Delegate

Do you take on more than you can possibly get done in a day because you don't want to ask others for help or don't trust that they can handle the task the way you would? That was me. I thought I could do certain tasks better than anyone else because I knew more about the task at hand. I thought it was easier to just do it myself instead of asking for help. Fear surfaced that it would not be done correctly or that it would be done better by the other person. At first, delegating was uncomfortable. When all was said and done, everything turned out great—slightly different from the way I would have done it, but done perfectly well nonetheless. And I had more free time for me.

I think back to how exhausting, stressful, and time-consuming trying to be Superwoman really was . . . and for what? When I learned to let go of control, I was surprised at how relieved I felt. Then I asked myself, "Why didn't I do this sooner? Why was I holding on to control so tightly? What emotions were underneath the resistance?"

Delegating helps promote wellness by decreasing stress and increasing more free time. Asking for help involves others and can foster trust, as well as bring a sense of community and unity. Here are some tips for when you ask for help:

- Let others do what they do and accept how they do it.
- Trust they will do their best.

- Be clear on the results you are looking for, set a timeline, and train them if necessary.
- Do not micromanage or have others check up on them for you.
- Let them know you are available if they have questions.
- Do not take credit for their work.
- Recognize, praise, and thank them for their contribution.

Elevate

Do you feel your energy level is low and your stress level is high? Are you attracting low-energy, high-stress people in return? Energy begets energy. I realized my energy was affecting the energy around me. What kind of energy was I radiating and gathering in return? The five years I spent slowly depleting my vitality, together with my near-death episode, took its toll on the body, mind, and spirit. I focused on ways to elevate my energy and higher-vibration emotions. Attracting positive, vibrant people and situations into my life was essential for my well-being and would need to start with me.

As I shifted my physical, mental, and emotional energy, the energy around me shifted. Maintaining higher positive energy protects you from being affected and pulled down by negative, stressful, and low-energy people. We all know people who are constant complainers or blamers, sad or depressed, or unhappy with their life. Know you have the ability to elevate your level of positive energy to bring yourself more in alignment with the joy and light of your inner spirit.

YOUR TURN FOR SELF-DISCOVERY

What changes do you want to make in your life to promote wellness? Reflect on the past year. What do you want for your life? Consider your roles, relationships, home dynamics, work environment, and finances. Look at the way you do things. Be aware of your habits, health, lifestyle, responsibilities, beliefs, fears, and limitations. Examine what changes you are willing and ready to make that will improve your health and well-being.

Self-Inquiry Exercise: Before you begin, find a quiet place and allow 10 minutes for this exercise. Close the eyes and take a few deep breaths to focus your awareness. When you feel relaxed and centered, gently open the eyes and begin.

On a fresh page in your journal, make two columns. Label the first column "Areas of my life where I would like to see change" and label the second column "Why NOW is the time to make that change. How will that change make me feel?" Then list three to five areas you would like to see change as you reclaim your life to promote wellness. Express why now is the time to make that change. Include how that change will make you feel. Here's an example:

Areas of my life where I would like to see change.	Why NOW is the time to make that change. How will that change make me feel?
Physical fitness	I've been sedentary for the past few months, and I'm starting to get achy. I know that being more physically active will help with my aches and pains. I will feel stronger physically and better mentally.
Social life	I haven't made time for friends because I've been so busy at work. My friends and I miss hanging out with one another. Spending some time with my friends will help me feel more connected and relaxed.

Nutrition	*I haven't been choosing healthy foods. I just get a quick bite here and there, and I find myself craving sweet, sugary stuff. It makes me feel lethargic after I eat it. Choosing wholesome, nutritious foods will give me more energy.*
Spiritual	*I've been feeling spiritually lost and this makes me feel uncertain and confused. I want to feel spiritually connected again and know my life has purpose.*

Your Core Values

When creating what you want in life, it's good to know your core values. Your beliefs, or values, are an acknowledgment of what's important, what matters to you in life. My five lessons included getting clear on my core values and purpose. Your values are the essence of who you are. When your thoughts, words, and behaviors are in alignment with your core values, you feel a sense of happiness and good about yourself. You are in alignment with your true Self. Living life through your values allows you to grow into who you want to become.

When you are making a choice in life, ask yourself if this action or thought is in alliance with your values. If not, then why would you choose that path? What purpose would it serve? Are you confusing one value for another? Is there an ulterior motive at play? If we get lured by distractions and detour from our path, we can feel disoriented. Once we get back on the path, staying focused on what's important and our direction, we move forward with more clarity, ease, and purpose. We live true to our higher Self. My values guide my choices and heartfelt decisions in my life. They act as my internal reference and support my greater purpose in life.

What are your core values? To give you an example, I will share with you my ten top core values that guide my choices and actions:

- Appreciation
- Caring
- Contribution
- Creativity
- Integrity
- Knowledge
- Love
- Playfulness
- Self-awareness
- Spirituality

Self-Inquiry Exercise: What matters to you in life? This exercise is designed to help you identify eight of your top core values. I've included a list of common core values on the following page. Choose from these suggestions and feel free to add any you do not see.

Before you begin, find a quiet place and allow 10 minutes for this exercise. To shift your focus inward, close the eyes. Bring your awareness to the breath. Breathe in and out through the nose. Follow the out breath to the end, noticing the momentary pause before you breathe in again. Let that pause be there. Let the breath complete itself. When you feel relaxed and centered, gently open the eyes.

As you first look over the list, write down in your journal all those values you feel truly matter to you. Think about all aspects of your life. Remember it's about your beliefs and who you want to become. Now, identify your top ten core values and list them in your journal.

Common Core Values List

Abundance	Discipline	Imagination	Passion
Achievement	Discovery	Independence	Perseverance
Adaptability	Dreaming	Influence	Personal Growth
Adventure	Education	Inner Harmony	Philanthropy
Affection	Empathy	Innovation	Playfulness
Ambition	Enthusiasm	Inspiration	Privacy
Appreciation	Equality	Integrity	Prosperity
Balance	Ethical	Intelligence	Purpose
Beauty	Faith	Intuition	Resilience
Belief	Fame	Joy	Resourcefulness
Bravery	Family	Justice	Respect for others
Calmness	Fearless	Kindness	Self-awareness
Caring	Financial Security	Knowledge	Self-respect
Challenge	Fitness	Leadership	Service
Charity	Flexibility	Learning	Spirituality
Collaboration	Forgiveness	Legacy	Strength
Commitment	Freedom	Love	Success
Community	Friendship	Loyalty	Teamwork
Compassion	Fun	Meaningful	Trust
Confidence	Generosity	Mindfulness	Truth
Contribution	Gratitude	Motivation	Understanding
Creativity	Happiness	Noble	Unity
Dedication	Harmony	Nonconformity	Vitality
Dependable	Health/Wellness	Nurturing	Wealth
Determination	Honesty	Openness	Wisdom
Dignity	Honorable	Opportunity	Youthfulness
Diligence	Humility	Optimism	Zen
Diplomacy	Humor	Organization	

In Closing

I was living from the outside in, believing that life's circumstances had caused my fate and determined my destiny. That thinking was backward. Here are a few key points to remember:

- Consider embracing inside-out living, where your focus is turned inward to connect with your inner wisdom to navigate your thoughts, feelings, and behaviors.

- Take responsibility for your actions and, subsequently, your life's path. It starts with a shift in mindset.

- Living your core values is powerful in helping to shape your decisions and who you become.

- Pay more attention to the power of your thoughts, beliefs, and consciousness, knowing that change comes from the inside out. As one of my clients so eloquently shared, "I now know that everything is created from inside me. My happiness and joy are an inside job."

I praise you for the courage to look inward and live from the inside out as you continue on your wellness journey of personal growth and development.

CHAPTER 3

Stress as an Opportunity for Growth

"Every crisis over the age of thirty is a spiritual crisis."
—CARL JUNG

Stress affects everyone and has become a global epidemic. I define *stress* simply as a biological and psychological response to any perceived threat that hinders getting what you want in life. According to the American Institute of Stress, 77 percent of people regularly experience physical symptoms caused by stress with fatigue being the number-one indicator. The percentage of people who regularly experience psychological symptoms caused by stress is 73 percent with anger and irritability being at the top of the list. Statistics show that 90 percent of chronic illnesses are stress related. The American Psychological Association's data shows the top three causes of stress in the United States are job pressure, money, and health.

Over the years, I've watched the symptoms of stress in people steadily increase. I see many carry out their daily activities habitually tired and frustrated. To add to that, the pressures of work, finances, and health can become all consuming. I observe the aggression of drivers on the roadways, the impatience between individuals, and the lack of physical restraint in disputes. I do not believe this way of life is to be expected. It does not have to be the norm.

Everyone interprets and responds to stressors individually. One person might become agitated or fearful, while another person is not affected at all. Why do people react differently? Our perception and thoughts toward stressors are based on the thoughts we have in the moment about the situation. They are influenced by our current mood and state of mind, previous experiences, and what we expect. Our response is also a choice.

Types of Stress

There are three types of stress: eustress, neustress, and distress. Positive or good stress, known as eustress, surfaces when you experience something inspiring and it motivates you to overcome a challenge. The thrill of winning a competition, job promotion, learning a new sport, or riding a roller coaster are some examples.

Our perception and thoughts toward stressors are based on the thoughts we have in the moment about the situation.

Neustress is neutral for it neither motivates nor harms the individual. It is where you learn about a catastrophic or disturbing event and react to it momentarily, even though it has no significant or direct effect on your life. Have you ever watched the news and felt stressed out learning about an earthquake, tornado, or hurricane? Perhaps you overheard a conversation with upsetting news about someone's child. These are examples of a neustress.

Another type of stress—distress—comes in two forms: acute stress that is short, intense, and then dissolves; and chronic, prolonged stress that leads to a multitude of problems. Examples of acute stress are getting stopped for a traffic violation, losing a business deal, giving a speech, having an argument, or the emotional rush from a free-fall drop from an amusement park ride. Once the intensity of the stress trigger leaves, the body rebalances itself. Chronic stress is of most concern. It includes situations like long-standing financial concerns, chronic medical problems, and relationship issues. Chronic stress hangs on. It drains the body, mind, and soul, which can break down bodily systems by continually triggering the fight-or-flight response. This makes the body more prone to illness. There is a correlation between chronic stress and health issues like high blood pressure, heart disease, obesity, type II diabetes, and depression.

Fight/Flight/Freeze Response

Walter Canon, a Harvard physiologist, first coined the term "fight or flight" in 1915. The freeze response was added more recently. When faced with a stressful or threatening situation, the body reacts with involuntary responses to adapt to the situation. The body responds instinctively, whether the threats are physical or emotional, real or imagined.

The hypothalamus at the base of the brain decides whether or not to react to potentially stressful events and then signals the body to respond if needed. The sympathetic nervous system is stimulated and activates the adrenal glands, causing the release of cortisol, adrenaline, and noradrenaline. This triggers the breathing and heart rate and blood pressure to increase. The blood moves away from the vital organs to the extremities, the pupils dilate, the body perspires, muscles tense, and the blood platelets become sticky to increase clotting in case of injury. During the fight/flight/freeze response, the immune system is suppressed. Oxytocin, the hormone that influences feelings, behavior, and physiology, is also released. It helps regulate the body and decrease epinephrine and cortisol levels, reduce fear, and increase relaxation.

This short-term, acute type of stress response is necessary for survival because it enables you to fight or run away. When the stressor is removed and the threat is over, the parasympathetic nervous system takes over and brings the body back into balance, or homeostasis. The recovery is usually quick and can take up to one hour.

The freeze response is also an adaptive behavior. When encountering a threatening or traumatic situation where the ability to win the fight or safely flee may not be viable options, a split-second, instinctive reaction is made to freeze. It helps keep us safe. There is the dreaded realization that there is no way out. You are rooted in fear and become immobilized or paralyzed, like a possum "playing dead." The freeze response can also be seen before or after a fight-or-flight response.

An example of the freeze response is seen in people who are sexually assaulted. Research reveals that a "relatively high percentage of rape victims feel paralyzed and unable to act despite no loss of consciousness during the assault." If you are witnessing a traumatic event, the freeze response can also be triggered. Another example is someone dangerously pinned by a car. They become frozen in time. They disassociate from what is happening as a form of protection and survival from the magnitude of the situation. The body releases endorphins to help reduce the perception of pain and attempts to adapt.

Men and women handle stress differently.

Stress and the Genders

Men and women handle stress differently. Have you ever wondered why men generally don't want to ask for directions when driving? Do you ever wonder how women can talk for hours about their lives or why women like "getting together with the girls"? In 2000, Shelley E. Taylor, PhD, and her colleagues at UCLA conducted studies to distinguish between the two genders' response to stress. Taylor's findings revealed that both genders react to stress with the same fight/flight/freeze response. However, there is one added difference among women.

During the stress response, the female body releases more of the oxytocin hormone than the male body does. Taylor coined this biopsychological mechanism, based in caregiving and support, *tend and befriend*. It describes the innate response women have to cope with stress by creating nurturing friendships and thereby a support system.

In primitive times, it was a means of survival and preserving the tribe. Women would bond together to both defend themselves and protect their children against attackers. Men fought and protected the village.

To help cope with stress, women turn to other women to create strong bonds, share their experiences, and nurture each other. They know they are not alone. Women who have supportive relationships with other women tend to have fewer mental, emotional, and physical challenges, and they lead happier and longer lives. To quote Jane Fonda, "Women friendships are a renewable source of power."

In contrast, men under stress are inclined to bond with other men through competitive sports or getting together after work to talk about business or current events, rather than their private life. It's not typical for men to discuss their personal problems and feelings, so as not to appear weak. Men are not void of feeling a myriad of emotions. Most men were brought up believing that it was unmanly to cry or show their emotional side. Therefore, they prefer to withdraw and be alone or remove themselves from the situation. I see this trend changing, as I observe more and more men beginning to have a shift in awareness with today's move toward more mindful living and being authentic. Some men are taking a chance in opening up and sharing their feelings. They are recognizing there is strength, not weakness, in truthful communication with others.

Stress and Wellness

We are all aware of the physical body and its functions. However, we also have an energy body. There are subtle energy bodies that make up the human energy system and interact with the mind, body, and spirit. These subtle bodies create a network of interconnected fields of energy surrounding the body, which is known as the auric field. The subtle bodies link with the physical body, directing energy through energy centers known as chakras. This energy is dispersed throughout the body through the meridian system (energy pathways), which will be discussed in more depth in Chapter 17. So what does this have to do with stress and wellness?

Stress and its emotions affect the human energy system. All illness and wellness begin and end in the human energy field. Our energy body gets damaged before the physical body is even aware of any adverse changes. Disturbances in these subtle bodies trickle down through the physical body and create disharmony. The chakras (energy centers) and meridians are disrupted. Vital energy and information the body needs get blocked, and this blockage interferes with the healthy functioning of the body. The energy field becomes weakened and imbalanced. There are interferences in the patterns of frequency of the functioning organs and bodily systems, resulting in illness.

Think of a garden hose. As the garden is being watered, if there is a kink in the hose, the plants will not receive any water and grow sick. Keeping our energetic pathways clear and balanced, in and around the body, is vital to wellness. Our current medical system is beginning to accept this fact. George Crile, Sr., MD, founder of the famous Cleveland Clinic in Cleveland, Ohio, has been quoted, "Diseases are to be diagnosed and prevented by energy field assessment." In 2017, "imbalanced energy field" was classified as a nursing diagnosis by NANDA-I, the North American Nursing Diagnosis Association International. This diagnosis means that there is a disruption of a person's flow of energy, leading to disharmony in the body, mind, and spirit. I believe many individuals can easily fall under this category.

When the body is on constant fight/flight/freeze alert, the body's energy gets depleted, resulting in the development of chronic disease. The nervous, cardiovascular, and endocrine systems are prey to the effects of stress. The nervous system shows the effect of stress through migraines, temporomandibular joint disorder (TMJD), irritable bowel syndrome (IBS), and coronary heart disease, which is first seen as hypertension. Dysfunctions in the immune system can result in colds and flu, allergies, rheumatoid arthritis (RA), ulcers and ulcerative colitis, and cancer.

This is why it's important to learn to recognize the signs and symptoms of stress and manage it before it evolves into chronic stress. Know what triggers your stress response and how the physical, mental, emotional, and spiritual bodies or aspects respond to those stressors. In the next section, you will have a chance to identify your stressors. Each person responds individually to stress and has different stressors in life. It's important to know *your* stressors. You cannot change that which you do not know is there. Learning how to deal with and clear stress is crucial.

YOUR TURN FOR SELF-DISCOVERY

Our perceived stressors can be our teachers, our opportunities for growth. Life comes with many teachers, if we are willing to recognize the lessons to be learned and the changes that need to be made to move forward in wellness.

Identify Your Stressors

It's time to identify your current stressors, your challenges, issues, and circumstances that activate your fight/flight/freeze response. As you identify each one, ask yourself: "How long has this stressor been affecting my life?" and "What areas of my life has it affected?" Some stressors may affect one or all four areas—physical, mental, emotional, and spiritual.

Self-Inquiry Exercise: Before you begin, find a quiet place and allow 10 to 15 minutes for this exercise. To shift your focus inward, close the eyes. Bring your awareness to the breath. Breathe in and out through the nose. Follow the out breath to the end, noticing the momentary pause before you breathe in again. Let that pause be there. Let the breath complete itself. When you feel relaxed and centered, gently open the eyes and begin.

In your journal, identify seven of your current stressors—the challenges, issues, and circumstances that activate your fight/flight/freeze response. Note how long each stressor has been a concern. What areas of your life (physical, mental, emotional, and/or spiritual) have been affected? Here are two sample entries:

Stressor: *Financial concerns*
How long: *One and a half to two years*
Areas affected: *Problems sleeping, nightmares, headaches, anxiety, insecurity, family arguments, overeating*

Stressor: *Heavy workload*
How long: *Four to six months*
Areas affected: *Difficulty focusing, unhappiness, tired, unable to relax, stomachaches, low-back pain, no personal time*

Signs and Symptoms of Stress

You noted which areas of your life are affected by stress. Now, listen to the body and notice the specific signs and symptoms of stress affecting your wellness. Be honest with yourself. Be aware of where your initial stress reaction occurs in the body. Start to become familiar with the body's sensations, behaviors, and state of mind so you can make a change.

Self-Inquiry Exercise: As you review the list of common signs and symptoms of stress as reported by the American Institute of Stress, record all that apply in your journal. As you review your selections, be aware of how stress is affecting your state of health and well-being.

- Frequent headaches
- Jaw clenching, grinding teeth
- Neck ache, back pain, muscle spasms
- Light headedness, faintness, dizziness

- Frequent colds, infections
- Canker or cold sores
- Rashes, itching, hives
- Unexplained "allergy" attacks
- Frequent minor accidents
- Heartburn, stomach pain, nausea
- Excess belching, bloating, gas
- Constipation, diarrhea
- Sudden panic attacks
- Chest pain, palpitations, rapid pulse
- Diminished sexual desire
- Anxiety, worry, guilt, nervousness
- Increased anger, frustration, hostility
- Difficulty concentrating, racing thoughts
- Trouble learning new information
- Forgetfulness, confusion
- Difficulty in making decisions
- Feeling overloaded or overwhelmed
- Frequent crying spells
- Feelings of depression
- Little interest in appearance, punctuality
- Nervous habits, fidgeting, feet tapping
- Insomnia, disturbing dreams
- Obsessive or compulsive behavior
- Reduced work efficiency or productivity
- Excessive defensiveness
- Constant tiredness, weakness, fatigue
- Frequent use of over-the-counter drugs
- Weight gain or loss without diet
- Increased or decreased appetite

Self-Inquiry Exercise: Now that you have listed your stressors and noted the signs of stress you are experiencing, take a moment to write in your journal any thoughts or insights this exercise has revealed for you. An insight occurs when something you once thought to be true suddenly dissolves and is replaced with a new thought. As you review your stressor list, notice how those stressors have affected your life and for how long. Write down what you observe.

In Closing

Stress can be an opportunity for personal growth and development. How you choose to deal with stress is a personal decision. Here are five takeaways to remember:

1. The top symptoms of stress are fatigue, anger, and irritability.

2. Women and men deal with stress in different ways. Women bond through supportive, nurturing, and protective friendships. Men bond, for the most part, through sports and social gatherings.

3. Identifying your stressors brings them into your awareness so you can make changes to remove them.

4. Stress and its emotions affect the human energy field.

5. All illness starts in the human energy field. Keeping our subtle energy bodies open and balanced supports wellness.

As you move forward in the next chapter, you'll have an opportunity to look at what it means to embrace and make a personal commitment to change. You will look at where you are now and your inner desires for change.

CHAPTER 4

Embracing the Concept of Change

"Embrace each challenge in your life as an opportunity for self-transformation."
—BERNIE S. SIEGEL, MD

Change is a choice. You can either continue on the same path or choose a new path and awaken to a new way of being. Are you ready to move forward? Do you want to be healthier, happier, and more vibrant? Does feeling calm and focused sound appealing? Can you envision your life filled with harmony and inner peace?

When I made the conscious decision to change and transform my life, I learned to make certain agreements with myself. The first agreement was to determine why I wanted to change. In Chapter 2, you identified the areas of your life you would like to change and why *now* is the time to make those changes. I also asked you to express how that change will make you feel. These self-inquiries help you get clarity to know your why. The second agreement I made was to make a 100 percent commitment to myself and my soul, as well as to my dreams and goals.

When you choose to embrace change, you may find having some guidelines helpful. Following encouraging suggestions can make a world of difference. Here are my fifteen guidelines for transformation:

1. Take steady baby steps so you have adequate time to introduce, practice, and integrate changes into your daily life with ease. As I mentioned earlier, it takes thirty days for new habits to form and ninety days to make it a lifestyle.

2. Have a beginner's attitude. Be open to viewing your world through new lenses, seeing things for the first time.

3. Be willing to learn, create new habits, and shift your mindset.

4. Allow yourself to be awkward with change. It's okay. Know it is part of the process. Accept it, love yourself for it, and move on.

5. Motivate yourself to keep going, especially when you notice old habits resurfacing.

6. Be willing to look inside for the answers.

7. Take 100 percent responsibility for your life. Living from the inside out maintains our freedom and power, eliminating the need for excuses and blame.

8. Trust your intuition. Listen to your gut or that little voice inside whispering and nudging you.

9. Surround yourself with people who support your desire for change and who are willing to be honest with you. Steer away from those who attempt to hinder your growth.

10. Find an accountability partner to stay on track as you progress. Choose an unbiased family member, friend, or colleague.

11. Be yourself. It's easier than trying to be what someone else wants you to be. Be who you want to become.

12. Praise and reward yourself along the way. You deserve it, and it will keep you motivated.

13. Be willing to take risks. Step outside your comfort zone.

14. Be able to evaluate yourself honestly. This is an ideal check-in system to track your progress.

15. Be grateful for the opportunity to grow.

Throughout this book, you are being guided through a process that will support you on a journey of self-awareness, self-care, and self-discovery. To fully embrace the idea of change, I encourage you to look at life from the inside out, letting your thoughts, beliefs, actions, and behaviors shape your world. As you do, you will begin to know yourself on deeper levels, perhaps like never before. Bring a sense of innocence to this transformational process by coming from a place of curiosity, openness, and nonjudgment.

As you move through your journey of transformation, I encourage you to open new doors and walk down new paths. At times, you may feel these principles are easy to follow and apply, and at other times, you may feel challenged to go that extra mile to reach your destination. Remember to believe in yourself and know that you *can* do this.

YOUR TURN FOR SELF-DISCOVERY

To begin the process of transformation, it's valuable to know your present state of mind and body. Getting a clearer picture of what you are feeling now and what you would like to feel can be very revealing. We can invite the unconscious and conscious minds, the right and left sides of the brain, to work together using expressive art and journaling.

Creative Journaling

Creative journaling uses art expression as a way to help you gain insight into your life. The focus is not on how good you are as an artist or how appealing it is to the eye. The emphasis is on self-expression and however that form appears. You can draw images, symbols, designs, shapes, words, and/or doodles. Don't think. Get out of your own way. Let your imagination come out to play and creative juices flow. Invite your inner child out as you play with the colors and discover more about you. As you look at your sketch, you are looking into a mirror that reflects your innermost feelings, whether it is frustration, anger, fear, pain, happiness, joy, or any other feelings that surface. Using this type of expression can be helpful during times of transition and when you are exploring new ideas.

This approach activates both sides of the brain. When you draw, the creative right brain's attention is on expressing your inner self—your thoughts, emotions, and feelings. Then, in the writing portion of your creative journaling practice, the logical left brain writes about your impressions. Both the conscious and unconscious minds are used for deeper levels of self-exploration and observation. In *Creative Journaling: The Art of Finding Yourself*, Lucia Capacchione, PhD, explains, "With words, it's easier to get stuck in the thinking mind. Rational thought is not where breakthroughs come from. They come through right brain processes that are not logical. Some people call this thinking outside the box." Are you ready to step outside the box?

My Approach to Creative Journaling

I use a large, spiral-bound blank book and colored pencils, crayons, and pastels. I open the book showing both pages so I can draw on the left page and then journal on the right page. In this way, when I am writing my impressions, I can look at the drawing without having to turn a page or move my arm to see the picture. If you are left-handed, you may want to reverse this and draw on the right side and write on the left.

Self-Inquiry Exercise: There are two parts to this exercise. You can choose to do them back to back or at separate times. Allow fifteen to twenty minutes for each part. You will need colored pencils, a piece of white, unlined paper, and your journal.

Find a quiet place with no distractions. To shift your focus inward, close the eyes. Bring your awareness to the breath. Breathe in and out through the nose. Follow the out breath to the end, noticing the momentary pause before you breathe in again. Let that pause be there. Let the breath complete itself. Notice any areas of tension in the body and invite those areas to release and relax as you breathe out. When you feel relaxed and centered, gently open the eyes and begin.

Part A

- How do I feel in this moment? Close the eyes and ask yourself this question. Bring your awareness inward and contemplate how you feel. Tune in to emotions, feelings, or physical sensations. Notice if any images, symbols, or words appear in the mind's eye.

- Then open the eyes. Remembering what was seen or felt, transfer them using any form of art expression: images, symbols, designs, shapes, words, and/or doodles. Arrange these images or words using any colored pencils you desire and placing them in any way you wish on the paper. Use the entire space.

- When you have completed your drawing, write your interpretation in your journal. As you observe your drawing, write about what you drew, including your reactions, impressions, and insights.

This exercise helps you to be present and get clear on what you are feeling. It's a valuable tool when you are not sure what you are feeling or what to do with those feelings. The following are black-and-white photos of examples of my clients' drawings along with their interpretations.

Client 1

Challenged with a physical illness, this client said her drawing represents feelings of hope and joy. The sturdy bridge over the lake is her spiritual path leading to a place she visits. Here she can laugh and swing from a tree in the warmth of the sun. She can watch birds soaring through the clear sky while listening to the chattering of squirrels romping through the tree. The large rock in the lower right area symbolizes her strength. She also noticed she drew the rock in the shape of a heart. Beauty and life is all around her with colorful fragrant flowers. The number of flowers represent the family and friends that love and help her. She feels the lake has healing powers. She can submerge herself in the water whenever she needs to rejuvenate. Her favorite spot to rest is beneath the tree where she feels grounded and safe, and where she can gaze at the water.

Client 2

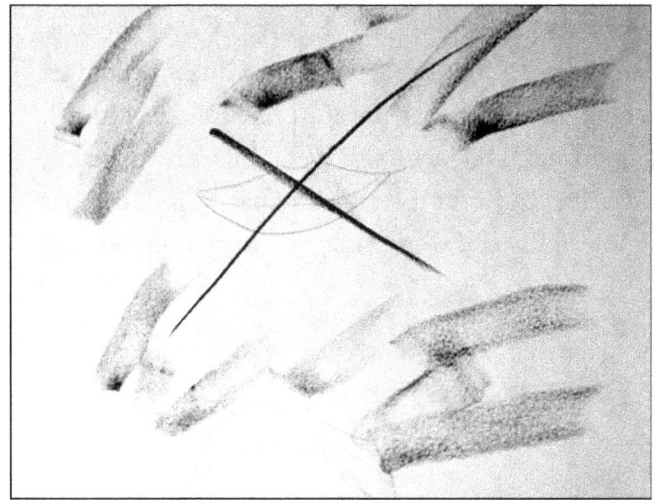

Drawing One

Drawing Two

In drawing one, the client commented she felt isolated and alone. There was no point in saying what she really wants because she believed no one would listen or take her seriously. In her second drawing, she shared feeling trapped and unhappy with darkness surrounding her. She saw no vision for her life, which brought her to tears. As you read on, notice this client's shift, as depicted in another one of her drawings.

Now you may either continue with Part B or choose to do so another time. Do not rush this exercise.

Part B

* What would your ideal life look and feel like? Close the eyes and ask yourself this question. Meditate on the question and let your dreams come alive. Look at physical, mental, emotional, spiritual, and environmental factors. Reflect on what you want, where you would live, and your interests and passions. Consider family and friends, home and work. Imagine everything flowing smoothly.

* Then open the eyes. Remembering what was seen or felt, transfer them using any form of art expression: images, symbols, designs, shapes, words, and/or doodles.

* When you have completed your drawing, write about what you drew in your journal, including your reactions, impressions, and insights.

This exercise invites you to create a vision of how you want your life to be and to explore the infinite possibilities that are available to you. No boundaries, no limitations—only your soul's potential. The following are black-and-white photos of examples of my clients' drawings with their interpretations.

Client 3

This client saw his ideal life as a target for success. The eight arrows represent the important aspects of his life. At first, he thought the words on the arrows were randomly placed. Then he explained the top arrow was about having clear vision with confidence and contribution on either side reinforcing his direction and purpose. He wondered why the lower three arrows representing family, love, and communication were on the bottom half of the target. He questioned whether the lower half was a place of less importance. This disturbed him because of his deep love for his wife and children. Then he felt all the words held the same value. As he continued to observe his drawing, he noticed money and adventure were on either side of the bull's-eye. It became clear to him that certain words were placed opposite each other for a reason. They were related and were a formula to help him achieve success. He interpreted his drawing to now mean that money affords him to travel; his clear vision is supported by his love of life; his family is where he gains his confidence; and his communication skills assist him in contributing to help others. He felt happy to discover he was already living his ideal life.

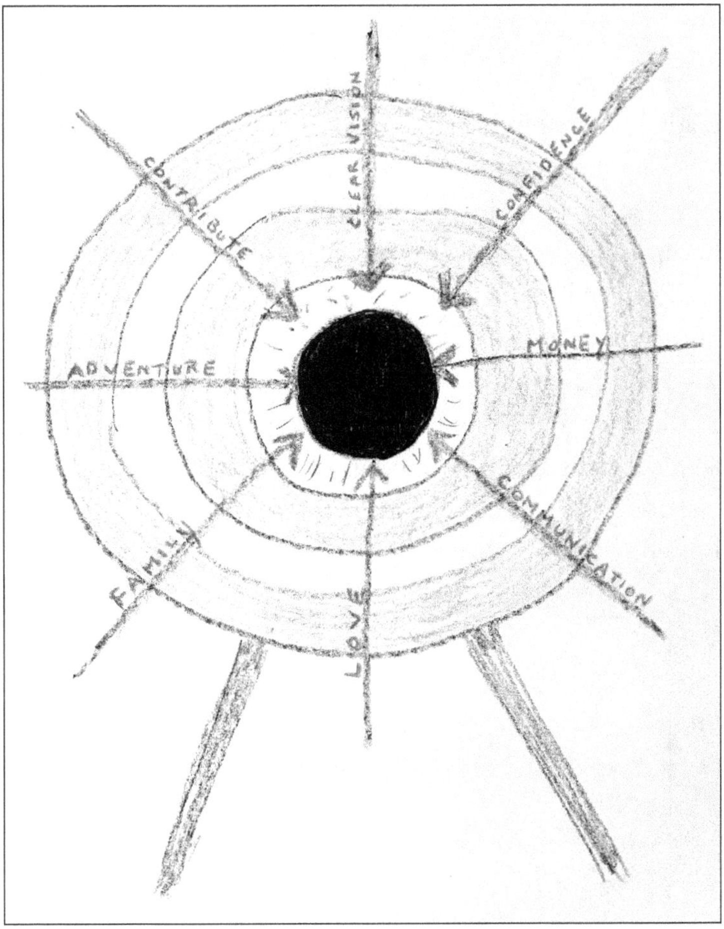

Client 2

After beginning to work on improving her self-esteem, Client 2 felt ready to draw her ideal life. Her multicolored drawing was one way she saw her life full of possibilities. She learned to meditate and wanted to include yoga to feel peace and quiet, as shown in the upper right corner of the page. The flowers, butterflies, and people holding hands in the lower right area showed she was willing to be open to love and friendships. The lower left space revealed the potential for growing new ideas that she can share with others for a clear and bright future. Travel by air and sea to exotic places was a newly found interest as depicted in the upper-left portion. She placed a heart in the middle area so love would be the center stage in her life.

Self-Inquiry Exercise: Now that you have explored how you feel and designed visions of your ideal life, it's time to bring your attention to any hindrances that may block your dreams. Before you begin, find a quiet place and allow 10 minutes for this exercise. Close the eyes and take a few deep breaths to focus your awareness. When you feel relaxed and centered, gently open the eyes and begin. In your journal, respond to the following prompts with your thoughts and insights:

- What roadblocks and obstacles (internal or external) or distractions may prevent me from living my ideal day?

- What steps am I willing to take to remove those roadblocks, obstacles, or distractions?

In Closing

Change is an adventure that requires you to commit to it 100 percent while being open to a shift in thinking. Looking inward and living from the inside out is where change begins. You can follow the fifteen guidelines on pages 36–37 for optimal results. At any point in your journey, if you have a question or are undecided about an area in your life, you can use creative journaling as a self-discovery tool to go deeper and gain insights.

Congratulations on completing Part One of this book! If you have been participating with the self-inquiry exercises, you have completed the following seven action steps:

- Become aware of what led you to the point where you wanted to change your life.

- Embrace your core values to guide who you want to become.

- Acknowledge the stressors in your life and acknowledge the readiness to make a change.

- Describe what your perfect day would look, feel, and be like.
- Recognize what is preventing you from living your ideal day.
- Commit to creating a lifestyle that supports your health and well-being.

Let the Journey Continue!

PART TWO

Free the Mind, Access Your Inner Wisdom

"Emancipate yourselves from mental slavery, none but ourselves can free our minds!"

—BOB MARLEY

Are you mentally exhausted, with so many thoughts in your head that it's hard to keep a clear mind? Do you wonder how some people appear calm even under stress, while you find yourself reacting with anger, frustration, or anxiety? As you continue along your wellness path, you will learn how to calm and free the mind from racing thoughts and mental clutter. You will know how to tap into your inner intelligence and wisdom to guide your decisions. By recognizing our roles and the dramas we play in life, we can refocus our awareness and be open to a harmonious life. When you deepen your spiritual connection from within, you feel a renewed sense of self. As you discover who you really are, you will know how to find the joy you seek. Intuitively, you know you are where you need to be right now to take the next step in your journey. Self-discovery is exciting!

After completing the practices and self-inquires in Part Two, you will be able to

- Understand the ego self from the spiritual Self.
- Have a meditation practice to quiet the mind and tap into your true essence.
- Rediscover the body's own inner intelligence.
- Learn how to decrease the drama in your life.
- Identify your four intentions to align body, mind, heart, and spirit.

It's not unusual at this point to start doubting if you can really reclaim your life. Do you worry about what you need to do or how you are going to do it? Are you wondering if the way you are living now is too ingrained to change? Let these thoughts pass through the mind without holding on to them. Remember that what you are feeling are just thoughts happening in this moment. Your thoughts are constantly changing, and you have the choice of what thoughts to latch on to and which ones to let go.

Some people pray for their situations to miraculously change so they don't have to do the work, and others wish for a magic bullet to dissolve their problems. Growth and change don't work this way. We need to take action. Remember your end goal. Embrace your vision of the life you want to live. Think one step at a time, and try not to get ahead of yourself. This is not a marathon to see how quickly you can get through these chapters. The point is to de-stress and be resilient, not add more stress and chaos to your life. Let this process unfold naturally. Pace yourself and stand in your power, knowing you create what you want. Let's begin.

CHAPTER 5

Accessing the Higher Self Is Key

"The Self resides within the lotus of the heart."

—UPANISHADS

In Part One, you learned about wellness and the effects of stress. I asked you to inventory your stressors and identify your signs and symptoms of stress. I invited you to embrace inside-out thinking and express your current life situation and explore your ideal life. You are probably aware of your present physical and mental health. What about your spiritual health? Do you believe it plays an important role in your overall health and wellness? Let's turn our attention now to your innermost self, this core aspect of you.

Spiritual Health

Spiritual health is a personal experience. Our spiritual beliefs can help us cope with stress and pain and enhance physical health. People who have a strong spiritual view on life tend to be calmer with less fear or anxiety. Connecting with our inner spirit assists us in finding meaning and purpose and adds value to our life. We feel a sense of harmony and inner peace. Spiritual well-being is enjoying life despite life's stressors and challenges and acknowledging our interconnectedness within all of life. It's essential to tap into consciousness for healing and wellness.

A little later in this chapter, I am going to share with you a present-moment awareness meditation that can prime you for your journey toward greater spiritual health. Even if you have meditated before or are currently meditating, I encourage you to be open to this process and approach it with the mind and innocence of a beginner. Meditation is a proven technique to reduce stress, access your inner wisdom, increase intuition, and connect with Divine Source, the origin of creation. Meditation is not a philosophy or religion; however, in every book of religion, there is some reference to meditation. It's easy to learn and effective at quieting the mind of unnecessary chatter, thereby increasing clarity and focus. It connects you with your higher Self and inner wisdom as opposed to relying on the perceptions of the ego self for direction.

The Ego Self

The *ego* can be defined as how one perceives one's identity and self-worth. We are born with no ego. First, we bond and feel a sense of oneness with our mother or caregiver. During our childhood development, if we feel loved, accepted, and protected and our life's experiences are positive, then a foundation for a healthy ego is formed. Our sense of self is being shaped. We are better prepared to go through life feeling resilient and flexible to life's changes. Self-confidence and self-esteem have a tendency to be high. We need the ego. It is not the enemy. A healthy ego is based in love.

If our childhood is filled with trauma and insecurities and these experiences are not given the chance to heal, then an unhealthy ego may develop. Unpleasant habits and behaviors can form. The ego may be filled with feelings like jealousy and not being good enough. Self-importance and always needing to be right are common traits. The ego responds to stress by being defensive and confrontational, when criticism and blame are used to control. When the unhealthy ego rules, it becomes the one in charge. These behaviors are hiding what's really going on inside. The ego self puts up a wall to protect us from the perceived fears and insecurities of the world around us. This wall can also hinder us from loving ourselves and our life. The ego says that we are separate from others and our environment. The concept of "us and them" is reinforced. We begin to see boundaries between our inner and outer worlds. Our sense of wholeness is affected.

People with healthy egos can also fall prey to the control of the fear-based ego. When we define ourselves by what we do, what we own, and the relationships we have, we are describing aspects of our ego self. We are creating our social image or persona, which is constantly changing. It is an illusion. We make it up. We take select pieces from what we do and have, package it, and present this image to the world as "this is who I am." The ego image we create for others to see may not give us happiness and inner peace. This can result in unnecessary stress, feelings of insecurity, and low self-esteem.

Do you remember the last time you went to a party where you knew only a few people? As you walk up to someone to introduce yourself, it's common to say your name, where you live, what you do, what you know, and who you know. In this scenario, you are describing things, people, and places. Those are the necessary roles we play in life, and we want to be good role players. However, it's not who we really are. We are not our egos. We are not our jobs, our accomplishments, or our material belongings.

As we identify with the ego and one of our roles gets threatened, we get thrown off guard. It can push us deeper into feelings of insecurity and uncertainty. How many people do you know who have lost a possession, a person, or a position and don't know who they are anymore or feel completely lost? We don't know who we are when we lose a role like this because we let that role define us. The ego kicks in, wanting power and respect and to gain control over the situation to have its needs met. At the same time, the ego self also lives in fear and seeks validation and reassurance. It's also very serious and gets offended easily. Keeping the ego's needs alive is exhausting and stressful. Letting go of the ego's needs to win and always be right is freeing. However, for some, there is comfort in holding on to the ego that uses our fears, doubts, self-criticism, impulses, and suffering to survive. It becomes a way of life. The distress is familiar yet filled with unrealistic expectations.

An unhealthy ego does not need to be a permanent ego state. It can be transformed by opening our awareness and developing a deeper understanding and insight toward our thoughts, feelings, and behaviors. Do our choices come from a place of harmony and honorable intentions? Are our choices aligned with our heart and soul's desires? Healing an unhealthy ego begins with the practice of caring for and loving yourself. What brings you peace and happiness? What inspires you? How can you honor the body? Are your core values and beliefs rooted in love? Do you celebrate your strengths and appreciate your shortcomings? When we take responsibility for our life and live with integrity, we hold the power to change and co-create our reality and destiny. We shift our perceptions to live our greater purpose. We trust and surrender the unhealthy ego self to the higher Self.

Lyn's Story

A client of mine, Lyn, complained that nothing was going right for her, which stressed her out. She had just gotten divorced and was renting an apartment. She wanted to be happy but felt like a black cloud was hanging over her. Bad luck would come her way, she said. She set out to get a better job and a place of her own. While interviewing for better-paying jobs, she overinflated her experience to, as she put it, "get ahead." One day, she was thrilled to land a new job that would pay her substantially more and allow her to buy a condo.

It wasn't too long before her happiness dissolved into worry. She was obsessed with how to keep her new position. She worked long hours and was praised for her extra push and being an example for others to follow. Once again, she was back on top feeling great. Then uneasiness set in again, remembering how she oversold herself to get the job. Her self-doubt and stressors took over, resulting in lack of sleep and not eating well. What would happen if she wasn't good enough and was let go? How would she afford her new place?

This is an example of living from the ego self with its fears and lack of stability. She was riding the up-and-down roller coaster of "I'm happy, no I'm not, yes I am, no I'm not."

After learning to meditate and maintaining a regular meditation practice for three months along with occasional spiritual mentoring, Lyn had a turning point. She realized her happiness was not going to be found while her fear-based ego ruled her every move. Her happiness was not the new job or the new condo. She now knows true, everlasting happiness comes from within. She accepts and loves having a healthy ego that is guided by her higher spiritual Self. When we shift our focus to the higher Self, our soul awakens.

The Higher Self

The higher Self is your true essence. It is often called the inner self, sacred self, true Self, or soul. It is the invisible *You*, minus the traumas and dramas. It is unchanging and timeless, always present and accessible. When we live from our true Self, we feel secure, centered, and grounded. We open our awareness to explore our inner self in relationship to the world. It is within the higher Self where we ask questions and receive answers, as we listen to the subtle positive messages and intentions.

The higher Self is where love and compassion, understanding and forgiveness, inspiration and creativity, and affluence and abundance are cultivated. It is where we access deeper truths and a deeper knowing. We are lifted up. Rediscovering the higher Self and our spiritual dimension is the key to higher consciousness. It helps us reconnect and realign with Divine Source. Your higher Self and Divine Source are not the exact same thing. You are the individual expression of Divine Source. It's like differentiating between a drop of water and the ocean. The individual drop exists in its own shape while also being a part of the ocean and not separate from it. Divine Source expresses itself through the higher Self. You just need to turn your attention inward. One way to connect with your higher Self is through meditation and being in present-moment awareness.

Present-Moment Awareness

Being present is being mindful. Present-moment awareness is a state of restful alertness to what is happening in the now. We open to present-moment awareness when we are not thinking about the memories of the past or thoughts of the future. That's where our stressors live. The *would've, could've,* and *should've* scenarios bombard the mind and stir up feelings of regret. The *what ifs* about the future can induce fear. Our happiness lives in the moment. Be aware, surrender, and accept the moment as it is. Presence is a place of freedom from anxiety and stress. Research shows that mindfulness reduces chronic pain, boosts the immune system, and lowers blood pressure while reducing the risk of heart disease. The more we practice being present, the easier it is to bring an alert, calm, and clear mind, along with a relaxed body, into our daily living. The following offers you several ideas for being in the moment.

Present-Moment Awareness Meditation

Before you begin, find a quiet place and allow 10 minutes for meditation. Close the eyes and take a few deep breaths to focus your awareness. You can practice all or any one of the following ways to be in the moment. Say to yourself three times, "I let go of the past and future. I am here now." Then begin.

- Tune in to the sounds around you. Don't analyze them. Simply notice and listen. How many sounds can you hear?
- Be aware of the breath moving inside you with each inhale and exhale.
- Pay attention to how you are feeling in this moment. Scan the body and be aware of any sensations.
- Open the eyes and look around the room. Take in all that you see, noticing the colors, textures, shapes, and space around these objects. Be aware of your place in this space. Feel the energy and space around you.
- Notice any thoughts that surface and let them pass through you without reacting or getting entangled in them. Observe your racing thoughts slowing down to moments of stillness.

Nurturing Self-Awareness

As you were practicing present-moment awareness, did you notice that you were only aware of what was happening at each moment? You were observing and being instead of actively doing. The mind was redirected to one-pointed awareness. I guided your attention to your senses and physical sensations. Being present is being in control of what enters your senses and what you respond to without judgment. It's where you choose to focus your attention. Self-awareness opens to self-discovery. You expand your awareness and feel more connected to everything around you. What I have learned is that when I am present, I feel calm, appreciative, and more at peace with myself.

It is possible to live completely in the moment when not even distractions can enter. Can you remember an occasion when you got so absorbed in an activity that you lost track of time and everything else around you? This happens to me often when I sit at the piano and compose music. I get into a flow. Two hours can go by in a blink of an eye. I am totally engaged as I let the sounds enchant me. My fingers seem to know exactly where to go as they caress the keys. I feel the depths of my soul in every note I play, whether expressing an air of sweet melancholy, ecstasy, or joy. My emotions move with the music like a sacred dance. I can see my story in the music. The music carries me to places within myself, opens the heart, and allows me to connect with Divine Source. I become the music and the music is me. I experience a sense of oneness, and I am at peace.

YOUR TURN FOR SELF-DISCOVERY

Now that you've taken a closer look at the ego self versus the higher Self along with present-moment awareness, you can discover how all of this applies to your life. Opening your awareness strengthens your ability to create change to move forward. There is an old saying that if nothing changes, nothing changes. Allow yourself the opportunity to change.

Self-Inquiry Exercise: Before you begin, find a quiet place and allow 10 minutes for this exercise. Close the eyes and take a few deep breaths to focus your awareness. When you feel relaxed and centered, gently open the eyes and begin.

Reread the top stressors you identified in your journal and what triggers your stress response. Bring into your awareness the role the ego self has been playing in your life. Recognize when you were reacting with fear-based emotions or the need to control. Notice when you were open to connecting with your higher Self with love and compassion. In your journal, share any insights or realizations.

Next, recall an occasion when you experienced present-moment awareness or being in the moment. What were you doing? What emotions surrounded that activity? What did you observe?

Share your insights in your journal.

In Closing

Our spiritual health is important for our overall wellness. It's a determining factor when it comes to coping with stress and our physical well-being. As we connect with our spiritual self, we find meaning, harmony, and balance. Chaos turns to calm. Tapping into a deeper sense of self, we realize our interconnectedness with life. The following are points to remember:

- Our ego is shaped in childhood. A healthy ego is rooted in love. If we learned self-worth and to feel secure and loved, the basis for a healthy ego was formed. Resolving childhood insecurities and traumas is essential for our happiness and well-being. An unhealthy ego can be healed. Self-love and self-awareness can transform an unhealthy ego into a healthy ego.

- Keeping the needs of the ego alive is draining and stressful. Letting go of the ego's need to control and win is freedom.

- True happiness comes from within. When you shift your focus inward on the higher Self, your soul awakens.

- Meditation is one way to connect with the higher Self and be in the present moment. It offsets the stress response while supporting the relaxation response.

- Present-moment awareness allows you to absorb the beauty of the moment while creating a restful, alert state of mind and relaxed body.

In the following chapter, I will introduce you to a self-mastery technique to access your inner wisdom. This meditation will take you another step closer in your journey of transformation.

CHAPTER 6

Finding Joy in the Stillness

"Meditation is the process of transformation and beautification of soul from a leaf-eating caterpillar to a nectar-sipping butterfly. It grows with the wings of love and compassion."
—AMIR RAY

When was the last time you sat alone in silence? I invite you to cultivate a deeper relationship with yourself. It's like connecting with an old friend you can trust and who knows you better than anyone else. It is a journey to greater awareness, creativity, and emotional freedom. It is essential in reducing stress. A regular meditation practice helps the body and mind function with maximum effectiveness. It is your passageway to living the joy you desire.

Meditation Makes Sense

When we meditate, we tap into our creativity, insights, and unlimited potential. We access our power and draw from our inner infinite wisdom and intuition to guide our decisions and actions. We don't react to every stressor that comes along or allow our stressors to separate us from our higher Self and Divine Source. Our perceived stressors do not change. What changes is our perception toward those stressors as we become more aware and present to see the bigger picture.

Some believe that meditation is too difficult because they cannot empty their mind of thoughts. It's the mind's job to think. The fact is, you cannot meditate without having thoughts. Thoughts must be there, so do not struggle with or try to stop your thoughts. It a fallacy that you will go blank for your whole meditation. As Dr. Deepak Chopra has stated in many lectures, "Meditation is not a way of making your mind quiet. It's a way of entering into the quiet that's already there, buried under the 50,000 thoughts the average person thinks every day."

People who crave a change may look to meditation for help. Here are ten reasons my meditation students originally came to me to learn to meditate. In their words

- Stop stressing out
- Sleep better
- Get a new life
- Improve my health
- Have more energy
- Improve my memory
- Calm my mind down
- Reconnect with my spirituality
- Help with depression
- Be more intuitive and divinely connected

Can you relate? Would you like to receive any of these benefits in your life? Then read on.

The Power of Mantra Meditation

There are many types of meditation, all equally powerful. Mantra meditation is a technique that can calm the restless mind and the multitude of thoughts known as the chatter of the monkey mind and release pent-up emotions. Mantra means *instrument for the mind*. Mantras are sound vibrations and the roots of language. When you silently repeat a mantra, it interrupts your thoughts without introducing more thoughts, so the mind settles down. A quiet resonance in the mind is created. In that quiet stillness, you tune in to your source for inner wisdom. It's like clearing the static on a radio and fine-tuning it for a clear reception. The mind is alert with a heightened state of awareness, as the body slips into a deep state of relaxation.

As you meditate, you go back and forth between repeating the mantra and having thoughts. It doesn't matter how many thoughts you are having or what you are thinking or how many times your mind wanders off. Whenever your attention drifts away from the mantra, you gently bring your attention back to the mantra, back to the present moment. Wherever your attention goes, it grows. If your attention is on trying to stop the thoughts, then you are going to think them all the more. Whenever you are aware of a thought, simply go back to the mantra. If your attention is on the mantra, then you stay present. For brief moments at a time, you enter the silent space, the stillness, between your thoughts, which is the entry point into your higher Self. You are accessing your true Self, which is silent. You are not your thoughts or your emotions. You are the one thinking the thoughts or experiencing those emotions. The real you is silent.

Remember, meditation is not a religious practice, and there is no need to alter or change your beliefs to practice. Many religions make reference to some form of meditation. Most spiritual traditions and cultures have mantras they sing or chant, such as *Hallelujah* (praise the Lord) in Christianity, *Yudh Hey Waw Hey* (I am) in Judaism, *Om Mani Padme Hum* (compassion) in Buddhism, and *Ishq-Allah Mah-Bud-Lillah* (God is love) in Sufism, and the well-known *Om* or *Aum* (peace and unity) in Hinduism.

The mantra I am going to teach you is the simple Sanskrit mantra SO-HUM from the ancient Vedic tradition. The sound *So-Hum* is the sound vibration of the breath. SO, or "That," symbolizes the universe and HUM, or "I Am," symbolizes oneness. This mantra represents, "I am one with the universe."

If you prefer, in place of the *So-Hum* mantra, you may either use I AM or simply follow your breath as you breathe in and out. It's your choice.

Susan's Story

When one of my clients, Susan, first learned to meditate with a mantra, she commented she had too many racing thoughts to meditate. She thought about everything from what she needed to do that day to memories of partying with friends, to dating, to worrying about work. She was struggling with her ego telling her to "stop meditating because it wasn't doing anything for her." I encouraged her to practice for one week and then decide whether or not to continue a meditation practice. After a week's practice, she found that using a mantra made a difference in her ability to meditate. Her racing thoughts slowed down and started to naturally drop away. Meditation seemed a little bit easier. Over time, she let go of her resistance and came to realize that meditation and being present just felt better. She was not "as crazy" anymore. Her chaotic thoughts simmered down, and she was more relaxed. This feeling carried over into her day. She felt more grateful and peaceful, which she said was noticeable to her family, friends, and coworkers.

Mantra Meditation

Prepare a quiet space to meditate with no distractions. (See Tips for Meditation Practice on page 63 for some helpful advice.) Allow fifteen to twenty minutes for this meditation. Silence your phone ringer. Set an alarm on very low volume for the end of your meditation time. You may record this meditation and play it back to follow along. Let's begin.

- ❖ Close the eyes. Sit in a comfortable position with the spine and neck straight and the chin positioned slightly down. Place the hands in your lap with palms facing up in a receiving position or palms facing down to feel more grounded.

- Scan the body and notice any tension. Invite these areas of tension to relax.

- Bring your awareness to the breath, as you breathe in through the nose and breathe out through the nose. No forcing. No effort. Feel the coolness of the breath enter the nose and the warmth as you exhale. Let the breath flow with its own natural rhythm.

- Now silently begin repeating the So-Hum mantra. Silently repeating SO as you inhale and HUM as you exhale.

- As you repeat the mantra, it may get faster or slower, or stop for a moment. That's okay. However the mantra changes, let it happen naturally without controlling it.

- Now listen to the subtle sound of SO follow the in breath and the faint sound of HUM follow the out breath. You may even hear the gentle sound of your breath.

- Whenever you notice your attention wanders away from the mantra, gently bring it back to the mantra.

- Have no expectations about your experience. Be easy with this practice. Continue to meditate for 15 to 20 minutes.

- Keeping the eyes closed, stop the mantra and rest in the stillness. Take your time to slowly transition back.

- Now, bring the hands into prayer position with a sense of gratitude and joy for this time you've given yourself. Slowly open the eyes and stretch.

Tips for Meditation Practice

Choose an area indoors away from clutter or distractions for meditation. I recommend you meditate for 15 to 20 minutes twice a day, once in the morning before breakfast or exercise, and once in the evening before dinner. If you do need to eat something first, keep it light. Eating or exercising beforehand can activate digestion in the body, which will activate the mind with more thoughts.

The morning meditation helps start your day focused, centered, and calm. The evening meditation helps you de-stress from the day, let go, and recharge. Meditation is your time to tune in and connect with your higher Self. As you develop a regular practice, you may find yourself wanting to increase your time from 15 to 20 minutes to 20 to 30 minutes.

Time your meditation. Test the volume on your device beforehand, so you are not startled when the timer goes off. Keep the timer close at hand so you can stay seated and rest after meditating. If you need to open the eyes to stop the timer, then only open them just enough to see. Then close the eyes again for 2 to 3 minutes.

When preparing to meditate, sit in a comfortable position. Use pillows if needed. It's important to feel relaxed. You can change your position at any time during your meditation. It's best to refrain from listening to music during this silent mantra meditation practice. Music will draw your attention outside yourself, stimulate emotions and feelings, and activate the mind, creating more thoughts.

During meditation, let the breath flow freely without controlling it or intentionally slowing the breath down. The breath will naturally get faster or slower as you repeat the mantra. Have a gentle attitude with your meditation practice. Do not judge your meditation. Just know it's impossible to have a bad meditation. Some people think they are doing it wrong when, in actuality, they are just not understanding the experience they are having during meditation.

Mantra Meditation Experiences

As you are meditating, you may find your attention stays focused on listening to the sound vibrations of the *So-Hum* mantra for the entire meditation. You are staying in present-moment awareness with the mantra. At times, you may catch yourself falling asleep. This just means you are tired. It is a good meditation, for it opens your awareness to your current state of health and well-being. Are you getting enough sleep at night? Are you eating healthy and taking care of yourself? If you find yourself snoozing with every meditation, you may want to look at your lifestyle and make some adjustments to allow for proper sleep. (I will be covering that in Part Three.)

As I have mentioned, thoughts are necessary in meditation. You can experience thoughts in the form of memories or being aware of noises or sounds. Being aware of any physical sensations (e.g., cough, itch, gurgling, discomfort) and emotions are also thoughts. When the body releases toxic buildup from stress in the form of any physical sensation, then the mind releases thoughts. With every thought or emotion, the body responds. The body and mind are one. Thoughts in meditation are an indication that stress was released from the body. Wonderful! It's important to not judge, analyze, or be concerned with the type of thoughts that come up. They are just an end product of releasing stress. The mind is dumping thoughts. It's good to know that lots of thoughts in meditation means lots of stress being released. Great meditation!

As you go back and forth between the mantra and thoughts, the thoughts and the mantra become fainter and fainter. Then suddenly, when you are not trying, the thoughts and the mantra disappear for a moment. And what's left? You, the silent one. This is when you slip into the silent space between your thoughts and connect with your higher Self. When you are in the silence, you are not aware of anything in particular. The body and mind are still and silent, while your deeper awareness is alert. Do you know when you are in the silence? No. You only know you've been in the silence when you come out of the silence. You may not even notice it happened. It's similar to when you stare off into space, and when you come back, you do not know what you were thinking about or how long you were zoned out. You tapped into the silence. Then, when another thought arises, you are back. These moments of silence are powerful.

All meditation experiences are beneficial. You want to approach each meditation with an air of innocence. No two meditation experiences are going to be the same. Each time meditating is different, so have no expectations. You will receive what you need in that moment. If you are to release stress, then you will have a lot of thoughts. If you are tired, then you will fall asleep. If you tap into the silence, then so be it. The only part of meditation that is important is how you end your meditation. You do not want to immediately open the eyes. It can be disturbing returning to visual and physical activity too quickly, especially if you were in the silence and a deep state of relaxation as your meditation ended. Take 2 to 3 minutes to slowly come back.

During meditation, the deep relaxation the body receives along with the quieting of the monkey mind is very healing. The meditation experience itself is wonderful. But it doesn't end there. The benefits are carried into your daily activities. A few of the benefits of a regular meditation practice are

- Less reactive behavior toward stressors
- Decrease in the body's cortisol (stress hormone) levels
- Increase production of oxytocin (love hormone)
- Less fatigue, more vitality
- Increased happiness, with more meaningful relationships
- Heightened intuition

- Improved sleep patterns
- Greater resilience
- Healthier brain

Stress is known to have a negative effect on the hippocampus, a part of the brain that controls the fight/flight/freeze response. We can reverse the negative effects of stress-related damage to the brain's nerve cells, or neurons: Meditation affects brain health by increasing new brain cell development and nerve cell density in the hippocampus. Through a regular meditation practice, we have the ability to change, grow, and boost the brain for a stronger, healthier brain.

Helen's Story

One of my clients got to experience firsthand the power of meditation. When Helen initially contacted me, all she knew was that she wanted to find a way to de-stress. She didn't know exactly the problem or what she needed to change and was clueless how to get to anywhere except where she was—stuck.

When she came to my weekly meditation group, she arrived tired and angry, did not smile, and most of what she had to say were complaints. Nothing was good. During meditation, she spent the entire time either fidgeting or sleeping, with a little bit of snoring. I was surprised to see her showing up every week. She expressed interest in learning the mantra meditation program I teach where she would receive her personal mantra. I instructed her two days later. She set her intention to meditate for 30 minutes twice a day thereafter. The following week she arrived at the meditation group a new person. Everyone, including me, was amazed with her sudden transformation. She was talkative, smiling, and happy. She meditated in stillness and stayed awake.

Two months later, Helen told the meditation group about an incident at her place of work. The retail store where she was a manager flooded. She said she handled the situation calmly and laughed at the predicament, which shocked her staff. Her ability to cope with the stress with clarity and humor surprised even her. The old Helen, as she put it, would have gotten angry and demanding and been miserable for days to come.

Even though her shift appeared rapid, her self-work had just begun. After working together with me for an extended period of time, Helen got clear and motivated about what she wanted in life and was determined to reach her goals. She experienced a major turning point in her life. She feels her shift was a healing miracle.

YOUR TURN FOR SELF-DISCOVERY

Starting a meditation practice can be exciting. This is the time to create a shift in your life. Are you committed to meditate once or twice a day? When you don't want to meditate is when you need to meditate. It's time to develop a meaningful relationship with yourself. Begin your meditation practice today. Enjoy the journey of self-discovery!

> **Self-Inquiry Exercise:** For the next week, keep a daily log of your meditations in your journal. Simply jot down a few keywords to describe the experience you had during your meditation (e.g., lots of thoughts, restless, slept, etc.). Then in a few words, comment on what your day was like, being mindful not to judge yourself (e.g., calm, hectic, tired, energized, etc.). Here's an example:

	MY EXPERIENCE DURING MEDITATION	MY DAY WAS
Day 1	Racing thoughts	Hectic, unfocused, had argument
Day 2	Calm and somewhat relaxed	Very productive, small disagreement
Day 3	Noticed some uncomfortable feelings came up. A lot of thoughts.	Sad, emotional, low key
Day 4	Kept falling asleep	Felt tired, no energy
Day 5	Calm, relaxed, less thoughts	Peaceful, fun, stress-free
Day 6	Back pain, many thoughts	Restless, a bit stressed
Day 7	Relaxed, peaceful	Focused, uneventful, no stress

In Closing

Meditation is an ideal way to reduce stress and connect with your higher Self. As we practice, the mind is calm and still, but alert, while the body is deeply relaxed. Meditation promotes health and wellness, affecting every aspect of our well-being. It is a self-mastery skill, allowing us to access our creative potential, inner wisdom, and intuition. Meditation is a journey of self-discovery with unlimited possibilities. Here are a few points to remember as you continue your practice:

- A mantra is a tool for the mind to bring your awareness inward.
- You cannot meditate without thoughts.
- Do not try to stop the thoughts.
- You are not your thoughts.
- Your true Self is silent.

- It's impossible to have a bad meditation.
- You will receive exactly what you need with each meditation.
- Be kind to yourself, and do not judge your meditations.
- Have fun.

If you found this practice valuable, at some point, you may wish to receive your personal mantra and tap into the sound vibration the universe was making at the moment of your birth. This powerful practice is taught in Dr. Deepak Chopra's mantra meditation program. I received my birth mantra twenty-five years ago, and it continues to be my main meditation practice. When I was first instructed, it felt like I went home. As a certified Chopra teacher, if you wish to know more, you may contact me directly at JanKinder.com. The program includes how to meditate with your personal birth mantra, how to perfect your practice, the types of experiences you can have, and exploring the seven states of consciousness you can experience.

CHAPTER 7

Discovering Who You Are

"What a liberation to realize that the 'voice in my head' is not who I am. 'Who am I, then?' The one who sees that."
—ECKHART TOLLE

Life is full of questions. Some can be answered outright. Some we choose to contemplate. Others need to be discovered. Tony Robbins says, "Questions provide the key to unlocking our unlimited potential." After my near-death experience many years ago, I could not put into words what had just happened or why. All I knew, at the time, was that I felt different. I had questions about my very existence. With much courage, some apprehension, and immense gratitude, I walked through new doors that lead me to several spiritual leaders. It was time to take a real meaningful look at myself. Through their teachings and my introspections and practices, I developed a deeper connection with my soul and purpose. I learned that how I see the world is influenced by my consciousness, mind, and thoughts. My self-awareness and personal growth evolved. I continue to share these insights with my clients. As you read on, discover how when awareness opens, answers to some of life's questions are revealed and whole new worlds begin to unfold.

Familiar Experiences

I noticed a common thread with some of the vacationing clients at The Self Centre, my mind-body-spirit and wellness center at Caneel

Bay Resort in St. John. There was a similar thinking and questioning among a good number of the baby boomers. It sounded like this: "I did home, family, career, and I'm successful. I did everything I was supposed to do. But what about me? Who am I? Why am I here?"

These major questions and concerns were included in the Centre's approach to wellness. Clients resonated with the spiritual mentoring, yoga and meditation, and energy-healing sessions that were offered. I created personal retreats for them based on their needs and desires. Relaxing on a beautiful island surrounded by turquoise waters and lush tropical vegetation made it easier for them to spend quiet time in nature and look within toward the Self. For many, it was a pressure release and a turning point. As I shared with my clients, "Going within means connecting with the light of our inner wisdom, which is our own consciousness."

As we have more contact with our inner wisdom and higher Self through meditation, our attention can grow and our perceptions can shift. We become more mindful of our life choices and conscious of our interpretation of the world around us. Every decision we make and action we take are guided by our awareness. We begin to experience different states of consciousness. Let's explore.

There are three states of consciousness common to all people. They are deep sleep, dreaming, and waking. During deep sleep, there is no dream activity, no muscular or eye movement, and no ego. The human growth hormone is released to nourish the body. It is suggested that the body and mind enter a deep state of rest and rejuvenation.

Dreaming or REM (rapid eye movement) sleep is needed for mental and emotional health. It is when the mind's imagination is activated with vivid dreams while the body releases stress and rests. Some dreams are nonsense; some are symbolic. Research speculates that during dreaming, the brain is organizing information and deleting irrelevant data while storing pertinent info.

In the waking state, we interact with images, people, and events. Everything is seen as real, including the physical body. We work and play for fleeting moments of gratification and amusement. We engage in thoughts and emotions, pain and pleasures. Even though we are awake, we still dream. The waking state is known as local reality for these visible and tactile things exist in space and time.

Do you live mostly in these three states of consciousness? Have you ever questioned if there is more to your reality? Are you ready to increase your awareness to the possibility that there is more to life?

Expanding Your Awareness

As we continue to increase our self-awareness, our mind expands and new perceptions become available to us. The states of consciousness grow out of our own experience. You may already have had glimpses of these experiences during your life.

In the previous chapter, I wrote about the deep level of silence you can experience during meditation. The mind is silent yet fully alert. You tap into an invisible field beyond the body and the five senses, beyond place and time. This field has no dimension, yet it contains energy frequencies and information. It is the experience of what is called nonlocal reality, meaning it does not have a physical location. The real you is not confined to the body. It is not something we can touch or see. Your true essence is everywhere, and it is silent. The real you transcends mind and body, space and time, and cause and effect. In his article *What Is Your Real Identity* for the American Institute for Vedic Studies, Dr. David Frawley's expresses, "You are the pure consciousness, light and energy of awareness behind and beyond body and mind." It is a field of pure consciousness or awareness, of inspiration and love. You've tapped into your higher Self and have a direct experience with your soul, your individual expression of the Divine.

As you continue to grow, the heightened awareness you experience in meditation crosses over into your daily activities. You bring your inner wisdom into the roles you play in life. You realize you are more than your ego roles. When this happens, the activities and life dramas do not take over and control you. They no longer cloud and spoil your happiness and spiritual health.

You also realize you write your own play and story. You choose who will be in your cast of characters and what parts you will play. What kind of play do you want to write? It's your choice. It's also your choice how you want to respond. You can step in and be the actor of your play or be the audience. When you switch roles and become the audience, you can detach and become the observer of the play. Being the spectator, you may even have a chance to watch a few comedies. One of my favorite ways of practicing this was at family or large gatherings. I had an entire host of entertaining characters to observe without engaging in any melodramas.

Knowing you are a spiritual being playing different roles can provide a feeling of freedom. "We are not physical beings having a spiritual experience; we are spiritual beings having a human experience." This quote has been credited to philosopher Pierre Teilhard de Chardin by various authors like Wayne Dyer and Stephen Covey.

Knowing you are a spiritual being playing different roles can provide a feeling of freedom.

When you experience a refined state of awareness, it affects the nervous system and the senses. It's a state of enhanced perception. You recognize the divine connection between you and others. You are aware that each person you encounter is a spiritual being who is playing out different roles. When you realize you are connected to everyone through the same energy source, you no longer wish to hurt or judge others. Forgiveness, acceptance, love, and compassion tie us together as one. You have a deep sense of appreciation for nature and its surroundings. The heart opens to the sacredness of every living creature. You wake up and realize Spirit is all around. There is a sense of joy and bliss being connected to the harmony and magnificence of creation.

As your awareness develops further, you realize that everything is interdependent and interconnected and merges as one. There is one universal and collective energy field that surrounds everything and makes up everything in existence. There is no separation between your inner contemplative world and your outer physical world. They are both connected as one. As British philosopher, Alan Watts, teaches in his article "Hermits in New York," which can be found at Awakin.org, "If you go off into a far, far forest and get very quiet, you'll come to understand that you're connected with everything." The inner world creates the way you perceive the outer world. We recognize Spirit in everything and every living creature. Your awareness, your consciousness, vibrates through and within all of life. This is a state of pure love and inner peace.

YOUR TURN FOR SELF-DISCOVERY

We create our own perceptions. As your meditation practices grows your perceptions and awareness also grow. It's not important which level of awareness you are experiencing. Self-discovery is at your own pace. Continue with your meditation practice, and approach it with childlike wonder. Become the person you were born to be and have fun!

Self-Inquiry Exercise: Before you begin, find a quiet place and allow 10 minutes for this exercise. Close the eyes and take a few deep breaths to focus your awareness. When you feel relaxed and centered, gently open the eyes and begin.

In your journal, share your insights about your meditation practice, even if you've only just started to meditate. What have you observed about yourself? As you observe and express yourself, remember self-criticism and self-judgment are ego-driven responses. Invite your inner wisdom to guide your responses.

You learned what is possible when your awareness opens. During the course of your life, can you recall having experienced a heightened sense of awareness of others or the world around you? Express these memories in your journal.

In Closing

Everything begins in conscious awareness. As our awareness increases, new experiences are available to us. As you have learned in this chapter,

- Deep sleep, dreaming, and being awake are common states of consciousness we all share.

- Through meditation, you are able to connect with your inner wisdom to explore more refined states of your consciousness. As you do, your heightened state of awareness is carried over into your daily activities, influencing how you play your roles in life.

- When you make a conscious choice to decrease the unnecessary drama in your life, you can increase the happiness, laughter, and joy.

- Self-discovery is an ongoing process. Remember, the real you is not trapped inside the body. Your essence is everywhere.

- Realize the divine connection you share with others. Recognize how we live in a world where everything is interconnected. There is no separation. Recognize Spirit in everything and every living creature.

Next, you will explore the power of words and how setting intentions can help fulfill your desires and goals. Living life with intentions provides direction and helps you focus on your core values in the present moment while adding meaning to your life.

CHAPTER 8

The Power of Intention

"Every journey begins with the first step of articulating the intention, and then becoming the intention."
—BRYANT MCGILL

Life is full of goals and intentions. Settings goals is about creating an action plan around what you want to achieve and sticking to it by keeping track of your progress. Goal setting focuses on taking actions for the future. Setting intentions is different. Intentions are declarations that focus on who you want to become. They help us shift our thoughts from limitations to positive and attainable solutions. The thoughts and words we choose for our intentions are important.

Words Can Influence

Words can motivate, inspire, and create reality. As you think, so you create. Your words have power. When you set intentions around those words, you influence your desired outcome. Intentions contain meaningful and productive information. We become aware of the actions needed to change and support our behaviors. Intentions are thoughts or principles that help us become clear about what we want and what we want to give back. They are inspirational, expand the mind, and open the heart to how you want to be or what you want to accomplish. There is a sense of positivity and encouragement of what is possible. They help guide your actions and behaviors to support a purpose and commitment to yourself and others. Your intentions are inspired by your inner wisdom. Setting intentions is a necessary and powerful practice that aligns your personal values and desires. Intentions are the underlying support in achieving your goals.

Leslie's Story

Intentions can help us in our decision-making process, allowing us to stay on track toward fulfilling our goals. This reminds me of Leslie, a client of mine, who wanted to lose eight pounds before her island vacation. Her goal was to feel comfortable wearing her bathing suit. Buying a larger size bathing suit was not an option. She had three months to create a plan. This was when she contacted me for help. To begin her coaching, I asked how she would feel about shifting her mindset around weight loss by creating some intentions. She jumped at the idea, saying, "I'll do anything if it works." Her intentions focused on nourishing her body with freshly prepared foods; avoiding sweets, breads, and alcohol; and burning fat by going to the gym three times a week. Over the next three months, she realized the power behind her intentions and relied on them to get her through to the end of her goals.

Leslie recorded her intentions on her smartphone, so she could reference them throughout the day. This came in handy for her. When her friends would ask her to happy hour or dinner, she felt caught in the middle. She did not want to shun her friends by declining the invitation or have them exclude her in the future. Reading over her list of intentions saved the day. She said, "It's like having my own rooting me on best friend with me." She was able to suggest alternate plans like getting together for afternoon tea or doing an activity that was not centered on food. That is exactly what happened. Leslie did reach her goal and had a fabulous vacation. Intention setting is now a part of Leslie's daily routine.

When was the last time you set an intention to do something? You can set intentions for that moment, the day, the week, or the year. Intentions can be big or small. We can set an intention around anything: What kind of day do you want to have? How can you bring joy into another person's life? How do you want your relationships to be? What kind of body to you want to have? Or what kind of experiences do you want to manifest? The list is endless.

Equally as important as clearly stating your intentions is being grateful when you receive the desired outcome of those intentions. Always asking for something without expressing appreciation is one-sided. In life when we receive a gift, it is courteous to say thank you. It's the same with intentions. Giving thanks when an intention has been fulfilled keeps the momentum flowing.

How to Set Intentions

Be realistic and flexible with your intentions. At times, your intentions may need to be changed or tweaked. Check to see if they are aligned with your beliefs and core values that you listed in your journal in response to the exercise in Chapter 2. Your beliefs and values strengthen your intentions and vice versa. They mirror each other. As you set your intentions and expand your belief in the possibilities, the quality of that experience changes. Energy changes with intention. Your focused attention around that intention is strengthened.

A great time to set your intentions is at the end of your morning meditation when the mind is more focused and clear. Record your intentions in your journal. After you set the intention, let it go. Don't try to force it to come true. Don't obsess over it or try to control the results, like the unhealthy ego will want you to do. Trust that everything will turn out the way it is supposed to. Let the outcome unfold naturally.

When setting your intentions, be clear in what you are asking. Ask for what you want and not for what you don't want. Stating what you do not want is vague. It says nothing about what you do want. Be specific. Speak only about your desires and not what others want for you. It's your choice; it's your life. Ask in the present tense and make it a fact, like it has already happened. You can start with, "My intention is_____." Here are a few examples:

- "My intention is to be in the present moment, both at home and at work, while being mindful as I interact with others."
- "My intention is to nourish the body, mind, and spirit with healthy foods, daily exercise, meditation, and a good night's sleep."
- "My intention is to strengthen and deepen my spiritual health and divine connection."
- "My intention is to consciously deepen my loving, fulfilling, and joyful relationships with myself and others."
- "My intention is to be mindful and appreciative as I share my work with flowing ease for the greater good."
- "My intention is to arrange undisturbed time for myself every day to do whatever I wish to do in that moment."

YOUR TURN FOR SELF-DISCOVERY

Are you ready to set a few intentions and get to know yourself more deeply? There are three self-inquiry exercises for you to do in this section. Let's begin with setting your intentions. If this is something you have done before, great. If you would like a little assistance, I'll provide that. You can use either one or both ways to set intentions. It's your choice.

Self-Inquiry Exercise: It's easier to set intentions when you are calm, clear, and relaxed, so create your intentions following your morning meditation. In your journal, write down three or four intentions. You may also want to write them on a small piece of paper to keep them near you when you meditate.

When you have completed your meditation, keep the eyes closed, place your awareness on the heart center, and silently voice your intentions. You may peek at the paper until you have them memorized. Focus your attention on *what* the intention is and not *how* to get there. Repeat each intention one, two, or three times, and then release it and let it go. Do not continue thinking about it. Once you set your intention, detach from the outcome.

If you need help coming up with your intentions, try the following variation.

Intention-Setting Variation: If you are new to setting intentions or wish to use a different approach, you may enjoy this process. Create a few intentions that you will use every day to help align the body, mind, heart, and spirit by asking yourself, "What do I want the body, mind, heart, and spirit to look and feel like to carry me through my day?" You can create your intention phrases by completing the following statements in your journal. Use two action words that describe each of these areas. You can choose from the list of action words provided or come up with your own.

The Body is (fill in blank) and (fill in blank).

The Mind is (fill in blank) and (fill in blank).

The Heart is (fill in blank) and (fill in blank).

I am (fill in blank) and (fill in blank).
(Describe your soul for this one.)

Action Words

- Awake
- Caring
- Creative
- Expansive
- Gracious
- Joyful
- Passionate
- Radiant
- Steady
- Alert
- Centered
- Divine

- Flexible
- Grateful
- Light
- Peaceful
- Relaxed
- Strong
- Balanced
- Clear
- Energetic
- Focused
- Healthy
- Loving
- Present
- Restful
- Transcendent
- Calm
- Compassionate
- Eternal
- Free
- Infinite
- Open
- Pure
- Soft
- Vibrant

Self-Inquiry Exercise: Healing and change start within the heart consciousness. This is where we begin to awaken, restore the body and mind, and transform our life. When we listen to the heart, we open to the opportunity to experience more love, peace, and joy. Intentions can inspire. Inspiration is a passionate and motivational force that propels you to grow. Your inspirations can influence what you want in life.

Find a quiet place and give yourself 10 minutes for this exploration. You can play soft relaxing music if that helps you shift your focus. In your journal, respond to the following prompts with your thoughts and insights:

- What inspires you?

- What encourages you, excites you, inspires you to move forward and take action?

- What do you find inspirational? (If a certain person inspires you, what qualities of that person do you find inspirational?)

- When have you felt a divine spiritual connection?

- What motivates you? (Perhaps it's nature, music, or love.)

Self-Inquiry Exercise: How often do you ask yourself, "What do I want?" When you express your wants and desires, it's beneficial to use phrases like I choose to have or I will enjoy having or I desire. By doing so, you are stating only what you want and not what you don't want. It allows you to be clear in what you are asking. Consider these aspects of your life: physical, mental, emotional, spiritual, environment, home, family, friends, and business. You may not know all that you want right now, and that's okay. Be patient with yourself. Desires change and grow.

Before you begin, find a quiet place and give yourself 10 minutes for this exercise. You can play soft, relaxing music if that helps. Close the eyes and take a few deep breaths to focus your awareness. When you feel relaxed and centered, gently open the eyes. Then in your journal, express your desires. What do you want? What's important to you?

In Closing

Intentions can inspire and ignite your fire within, and change your life. They motivate you to get clear about where you want to go and how you want to get there. Setting intentions helps bring your goals to fruition. When setting intentions, remember:

- Setting intentions aligns your personal values and desires.
- Set your intentions after meditation when the mind is more focused.
- Ask for what you want and not for what you don't want.
- Use words to state your intention as though it has already happened.
- Be thankful for receiving what you wanted.
- Intentions can inspire and move you forward in your personal growth.

Congratulations on completing Part Two of this book. You have received a meditation practice with setting intentions to empower your day. You have become clearer on what inspires you and what you want and desire for your life at this time. Moving forward, you will learn the ins and outs of how to create a great day, every day. Are you ready?

You are on your way!

PART THREE

Daily Rituals for a Healthier You

"You will never change your life until you change something you do daily. The secret of your success is found in your daily routine."
—JOHN C. MAXWELL

Is your schedule so busy that you put off taking care of yourself until you have some free time? Do you overload your day so much that you are always "doing" or producing something? Does your inner child get some time to simply play and have fun each day? Do you want to orchestrate your life so that you can spend less time distressing and do more of what makes you happy? If so, you are ready to get back in sync with life.

As you take your next steps forward, you will learn how to develop a doable daily schedule that promotes vibrant health and well-being and a sense of wholeness. I will lead you through stress-reducing skills and approaches that you can apply immediately to your life. You will learn how to develop your own unique relaxation plan and suggestions for a restful night's sleep. You will also learn how to live a day with more ease. After completing the practices and self-inquiries in this part, you will be able to:

- Integrate new healthy habits into your existing schedule with ease.
- Know how to start and end your day focused, balanced, and calm.
- Use simple, effective coping strategies and skills to resolve issues and promote peace of mind.
- Experience the breath and imagery as powerful tools to de-stress.
- Create your personal relaxation plan to interrupt the stress response and restore balance.

The information, practice, and techniques I share in this part are where your journey with me begins to take shape and comes to life. You will learn the guidelines and blueprint I have used in my life for decades.

CHAPTER 9

Aligning Your Biological Rhythms

"We have made clocks that are perfectly in sync with the industrial machinery and the Information Age and perfectly out of sync with nature and our circadian rhythm."
—KHANG KIJARRO NGUYEN

Years ago, before electricity, we followed the rhythms of nature. We went to sleep soon after dark and awoke with the morning sun. When the sun was high in the sky around the noon hour, we ate our main meal to refuel the body. We finished our work and ate a light supper before slowing down in preparation for sleep. We slept at least eight hours and started the day rested and energized.

The body was designed to function in alignment with our biological rhythms. One of those rhythms is the 24-hour internal clock known as the circadian rhythms. These rhythms are controlled by a small area of the hypothalamus part of the brain. They affect sleep-wake cycles, hormone production, cell regeneration, and influence bodily functions like breathing, hunger, digestion, and elimination.

Circadian rhythms structure our day. In today's hectic world, it's more challenging to follow a daily routine that promotes wellness and well-being. When you don't get enough sleep at night due to anxiety, stress, or working late, your whole day can get thrown off schedule in more ways than one. If these daily rhythms are constantly disturbed, we get out of balance, out of sync, and health issues can surface. Continual disruption of our circadian rhythms can result in chronic problems like diabetes, obesity, cardiac issues, depression, insomnia, and cognitive impairment.

To maintain optimal health, it's essential to create daily wellness practices that are integrated throughout the day to get our internal clock back in rhythm with nature. Integration was an important self-care principle I learned from my near-death experience. Before, I used to wait until the weekend or the end of the day to de-stress. Obviously, that did not work for me in the long run. As I teach my clients, it's necessary to keep yourself balanced, relaxed, and centered throughout the day, and not wait. Waiting can release stress hormones, exhaust the mind, and drain the body. We need to recognize our stressors and release the effects of that stress as it arises. I will provide you with ways to do that in Chapter 11. For now, you will learn the value of integrating wellness practices or healthy habits into your daily life. I encourage clients to treat these health-based practices like rituals. Rituals encourage self-awareness and help you connect on a deeper, more insightful level with yourself. Daily habits are turned into something sacred and meaningful.

Daily Rituals

The daily rituals discussed next have proven effective for a happier and healthier life for my clients, as well as for me for well over two decades. These practices provide a way to start your day alert, centered, and focused, and end your day calm, relaxed, and grateful. Along with current integrative wellness practices, many of the principles I will share are based in the ancient and preventive health system known as Ayurveda (pronounced *I-your-vay-da)*, or the science of life.

Before we start, let me point out that you do not have to change your lifestyle in a day or two. Ease into this. You may find you are already following some of these simple and powerful habits and reaping the benefits. Your change may be in your mindset. If this information is new to you, choose which practices you want to begin now, and then add the other over the next week or two. As you introduce these practices into your life, know that it takes 30 days to create a new habit, and 90 days to make that habit a part of your lifestyle so that it becomes a way of life.

Morning Rituals

Wake up. Get in the habit of waking up at the same time every day, including weekends. According to Ayurveda, the ideal time is between 5 and 6 a.m. Your bodily functions will get moving and flow better with a consistent routine. Waking up gently and calmly is preferred. When we are jolted awake by a loud alarm clock, we get startled and our fight-flight-freeze response is triggered. This is no way to start your day. It's no wonder we call it an "alarm" clock. If you are not able to wake up naturally, use an alarm clock specifically designed to wake you peacefully.

Meditate. How you start your day sets the pace for the rest of your day. Spend 15 to 20 minutes meditating as soon as you wake up before you do anything else. You may want to empty your bladder and brush your teeth and clean your tongue first. If your toothbrush does not have a tongue scraper on the reverse side of the brush head, you can purchase one.

I find it's easier to meditate as soon as I wake up instead of getting my day going and then have to stop to meditate. There may be fewer distractions at this hour, too. I have found this to be a key factor for a successful practice. Experiment and see what will work best for you.

Drink warm lemon water. Begin your day hydrated. Mixing lemon juice, a great source of vitamin C, with warm water helps flush out toxins and stimulates the bowels.

Move it or lose it. In the morning, the body's metabolism is slower, so it's a good time to get the body moving. Choose an activity you enjoy and make exercise fun. Yoga, qigong, or tai chi are ways to exercise as well as develop self-awareness. These practices cultivate calmness, manage the flow of your life force energy (*qi* or *chi*), help correct imbalances, and strengthen the body. You can exercise by dancing, working out, or with brisk walking. Participate in walk-a-thons in your neighborhood and include your friends for added fun.

If an exercise regimen is new for you, and you don't feel like you have enough time to exercise, start with 10 minutes three times a week. Then increase the time by 5 minutes every two weeks until you reach a 30-minute workout. Gradually over 10 weeks, you will be exercising 30 minutes three times a week. Exercise is also beneficial for good sleep hygiene.

Bathe. What you put on the skin, the largest organ of the body, is absorbed directly into the body. Plus, hot water opens the skin's pores and increases the absorption. To that end, you may want to avoid soaps, bath wash, bath oils, and shampoos that contain substances known to be harmful. Two ingredients I steer clear of are sodium lauryl sulfate/sodium laureth sulfate (used as a foaming agent) and parabens (preservatives), which disrupt hormones and can mimic estrogen. I use plant-based products that do not contain artificial colors, petroleum, chemical preservatives, or any other questionable ingredients.

Eat breakfast. Ayurveda suggests starting your day with a light yet filling breakfast around 8 a.m. Listen to the body and decide if it wants food or not. Some people do not need food until later in the morning around 10 a.m. or lunchtime. If you have a medical condition that requires you to eat, then eat. To help fuel your metabolism, it is best to sit down to eat and use your energy for digestion and burning calories. A lean protein, low-fat breakfast will help build muscle, satisfy you, and help you feel fuller, longer.

Afternoon Rituals

Midday is when your ability to digest food is the strongest. Eating your main meal of the day during the lunch hour is ideal. It was how the body was designed. I suggest you take a brief and brisk walk right after your meal. This will aid in your metabolism and digestion, and help you avoid feeling heavy or sluggish. You can manage your physical energy throughout the day by moving the body during work breaks, parking your car on the far side of the parking lot and walking, and choosing stairs over elevators.

Evening Rituals

Before preparing your dinner, you may choose to let go and relax with some meditation, even if for only 10 minutes. It will calm the body and aid in your digestion. It's important to be with family or friends and feel refreshed. During the evening hours, the body's metabolism begins to slow down. Eating a large meal for dinner is not necessary. You do not need that much food at night, so you want to eat less and finish by 7 to 7:30 p.m. or three hours before sleep.

It takes three hours for the majority of the ingested food to leave the stomach, and five to six hours to be digested. Trying to go to sleep on a full stomach disrupts your sleep cycle. The body gets mixed messages. Is it supposed to be actively digesting a meal or is it to be resting, so the body can remove toxins and rebuild cells and tissues? If the body is busy digesting a late-night dinner, then the body cannot fully detox and rejuvenate. This process occurs between the hours of 10 p.m. and 2 a.m., so we also want to be asleep for most of those hours.

What to Eat

First, if you have special nutritional needs, I recommend you consult with a registered dietitian or your doctor. Now, about food basics. It's been said, "You are what you eat." It's vital to be informed about what kinds of food support health and wellness. You may already be applying this information to your food choices. Here are some pointers:

* Eat freshly prepared food as often as possible.

* Know which foods are right for you. The body will respond, so pay attention; feel and listen to your inner wisdom. It's okay if you are not a vegetarian or vegan. Not all people choose these lifestyles.

* When possible, choose organic fruits and vegetables. If you are not able to eat organic, you may find it helpful to know which foods contain a high concentration of pesticides. The Environmental Working Group Organization (EWG) has shared a list of those foods. The following are known as the Dirty Dozen and the Clean Fifteen.

DIRTY DOZEN (Buy Organic)		CLEAN FIFTEEN (Can Choose Non-Organic)	
Strawberries	Spinach	Avocados	Sweet Corn
Nectarines	Apples	Pineapples	Cabbage
Grapes	Peaches	Onions	Sweet peas (frozen)
Cherries	Pears	Papayas	Asparagus
Tomatoes	Celery	Mangoes	Eggplants
Potatoes	Sweet Bell Peppers	Honeydew Melons	Kiwis
		Cantaloupes	Cauliflower
		Broccoli	

* If you consume dairy, it's good to know that with organic dairy products, cows are not treated with synthetic hormones or antibiotics. The cows graze on food that has been grown without pesticides or genetically modified seeds (GMO).

* If you eat eggs, find a local farmer or choose organic pasture-raised

eggs where the hens forage on what nature intended like green plants, earthworms, insects, and wild seeds.

- If you consume meat, pick free-range chickens not treated with hormones or antibiotics. Choose grass-fed beef that is also grass finished, which means the cows were grazed on grass and no grains for their entire life.
- Choose wild caught fish.
- Limit your intake of refined sugars. Studies show high-sugar diets can increase the risk of obesity, diabetes, heart disease, and cancer. Read food labels and be aware of the sugar content. Observe how much of your daily intake is sugar and which foods you are willing to let go of.
- Lower your stress levels and feed the brain with de-stressing foods like blueberries, walnuts, and dark chocolate that is 70 percent or more cacao.
- When it comes to vitamins, I encourage you to check with your health-care provider about what's appropriate for you. Be sure to have your doctor check your vitamin D levels.
- Use spices and herbs like cinnamon, sage, and turmeric to aid digestion and improve health.
- Fats are essential for heart health, brain function, and healthy skin. The seven ideal fats are 1) extra virgin olive oil, 2) almonds, 3) walnuts, 4) flax seeds, 5) chia seeds, 6) avocado, and 7) ghee (clarified butter; it is lactose and casein free).

How to Eat

I have a mantra that I say before I eat. It's a favorite among my clients, too. "Everything I eat turns to health and beauty." It works exceptionally well when I choose to indulge in something sweet. It eliminates the guilt and stress, which can be worse than eating the food.

How we eat is as important as *what* we eat. I've listed nine Ayurvedic tips on how to improve your digestion and extract more nutrients from your food. Notice which of these behaviors you are already doing and which you aren't. Pick a few you would like to explore and practice. Jot those down in your journal as a reminder. Eventually, you may want to consider adding all of them. The body will thank you.

- Eat in a relaxing, quiet atmosphere with soft, pleasing music and/or nourishing conversation.
- Be mindful and pay attention to what you are eating. Enjoy the tastes, textures, and colors of the food. Distractions like watching television or being on electronic devices rob you of truly enjoying your food.
- Eat your main meal during lunchtime hours. Your digestive system is the strongest during midday.
- Eat dinner at least three hours before bedtime, so your stomach is mostly empty before sleep.
- Do not eat when you are upset. Stress hormones, like cortisol, get released and disrupt your digestion. Take a few breaths and relax, and allow more pleasant thoughts to enter the mind, which will create calmer feelings.
- Reduce your intake of ice-cold beverages right before, during, and after you eat. Ice-cold fluids numb the taste buds, contract the blood vessels, and disturb fat absorption. The cold shocks the body and interferes with its ability to digest and absorb necessary nutrients. The body's energy is redirected to regulate body temperature. Imagine on a cold morning you are snuggled in bed under the warm covers. Now, someone rips off those covers and throws ice water on you. How do you think the body will react? It will tense up,

then take a while to warm up again. Ice water can also solidify the ingested fats, leaving unwanted fat deposits in the intestinal tract. Sipping room temperature or warm water with lemon or warm tea throughout your meal is a great way to help break down the food, increase your metabolic rate, and enhance your digestion.

- Do not rush your meal. Eating at a slower pace results in better absorption and can help with weight loss. It takes about 20 minutes for the brain to register that you are full. When you eat too fast, you miss this trigger and can overeat. The stomach needs some empty space to properly and fully digest the food. Slower eating invites us to chew and savor every morsel in a calm and relaxed manner.
- Take a walk after eating to aid metabolism and digestion.
- Stay well hydrated. Keep a water bottle with you and drink throughout the day.

Hydration Is the Fountain of Youth

Drinking water seems the most obvious thing to do, yet many adults experience mild or moderate dehydration and don't even know it. It's common to lose fluids when you are exercising or during the warmer climate months. However, you can get just as dehydrated in colder climates or at higher altitudes. The skin loses moisture when exposed to these environments. Also, living in artificially heated environments can be drying, creating even more loss of fluid.

More than half the body's weight is made up of water. Besides oxygen, every cell, tissue, and organ, including the brain, needs water to function and survive. I remember my microbiology professor in nursing school, a short woman with large, circular, thick-rimmed glasses, teaching, "When it dries, it dies." Her words ring true.

Dehydration results in the loss of necessary electrolytes from the body. The cells and tissues do not receive enough fluid to function adequately. A lack of fluids can cause overall fatigue, joint and muscular discomfort, dryness of the lips and mouth, brain fog, and lightheadedness.

It is vital that your skin, the body's largest organ, receive proper hydration to prevent the skin from drying out causing wrinkles and premature aging. Keeping the body adequately hydrated helps create more youthful and firmer skin.

Hunger or Thirst?

It's important to know the difference between when you are hungry and when you are thirsty. At times when we are feeling light-headed or tired, we tend to reach for food but, in actuality, we are really only thirsty. Under stress, we may also eat for emotional comfort and ignore the signals of thirst altogether. Quenching your thirst may prevent you from overeating. A good check system is this: If you think you're hungry, drink a glass of water first and wait 5 to 10 minutes. Then, if you are still hungry, eat.

How Much to Drink?

The amount of fluids you need to consume varies from person to person. In general, it is recommended to drink half your body weight in ounces. For example, if you weigh 140 pounds, you will consume 70 ounces of water a day. It's crucial to drink throughout the day before your thirst builds up. Waiting until you are thirsty to drink is a sign you are already dehydrated.

Be aware and listen to the body's signals. Our internal thirst meter will let us know how much water we need. We also need to use common sense to stay well hydrated when we are losing fluids, as when we are sick with fever, vomiting, or experiencing loose stools.

Pure filtered water is the best source of fluids. For those who find water less than appealing, try flavoring it with real fruit or herbs. My favorite is a refreshing blend of raspberry, lemon, and cucumber. Keep water with you, and drink steadily throughout the day. I prefer to fill my own glass bottles with fruit-infused water, instead of drinking from plastic bottles. I know the source of my water and where it gets its flavor from. Plus, it feels good that I'm helping the environment with less plastic waste.

Here are two simple ways to check if you are taking in enough fluids:

- Are you urinating every three to four hours? If not, you are not drinking enough.
- What is the color of your urine? Healthy urine is a pale straw or transparent yellow color. Dark yellow or amber is a sign you need to drink water as soon as possible. It's also important to note that certain foods, vitamins, medications, and illnesses can change the color of your urine. Always check with your health-care provider if your urine is consistently dark, even after increased hydration.

A final note: If you are concerned about whether or not your fluid intake is adequate, it is best to ask your health-care provider the recommended amount of fluids that are appropriate for you, taking into consideration any health concerns, such as congestive heart failure, diabetes, or kidney problems, that may be a contributing factor.

YOUR TURN FOR SELF-DISCOVERY

Has any of the information in this chapter changed your way of thinking about your daily schedule? Are there any changes you are ready to make concerning when you eat and what and how you eat? I prompted you earlier to choose which practices or changes you want to begin now, and then add the others over the next week or two. Go easy on yourself with this.

Self-Inquiry Exercise: Before you begin, find a quiet place and allow 10 minutes for this exercise. Close the eyes and take a few deep breaths to focus your awareness. When you feel relaxed and centered, gently open the eyes and begin. In your journal, write what you are willing to commit to in the following areas:

Daily Rituals	**Eating and Hydration**
Morning Ritual	What to Eat
Afternoon Ritual	How to Eat
Evening Ritual	Hydration

In Closing

A daily routine is essential if you want to improve or maintain wellness. Become a conscious eater and choose nourishing, freshly prepared foods. Consuming food is a sacred celebration where the body is treated like a temple. Drinking fluids throughout the day is essential in maintaining adequate functioning of the bodily systems and staying healthy. Here are some points to remember:

- How you start your day affects the rest of your day.
- Daily rituals initially start out as a task to try, then soon become a habit followed by a sustainable lifestyle behavior.
- Habits help provide structure and stability to life. They organize daily activities to allow for more focused energy that translates into a more productive life.
- Your eating rituals are vital for extracting the most nutrients for adequate energy and stamina. What, when, and how you eat all play a part in supporting your health and well-being.
- Stay well hydrated; remember, if you are very thirsty, you are already dehydrated.

✤ Being aware and listening to the body's signals will help guide you in nourishing yourself.

Now that you know how to create an ideal daily routine for optimal health, the following chapter will teach you how to get a better night's sleep and wake up refreshed and energized.

CHAPTER 10

Letting Go of the Day

"Sleep is the best meditation."
—DALAI LAMA

When was the last time you slept seven or eight hours and woke up refreshed, energized, and ready to go? Or are you one of the 45 percent of Americans who suffer from sleep deprivation, as reported by the Sleep Health Index™ developed by the National Sleep Foundation? We all have occasional nights when our sleep gets disturbed. However, when our lack of sleep becomes chronic, there is cause for concern.

Stress can lead to insomnia. The primary reason is related to emotional stress and our ability to turn off the mental chatter enough to naturally drift off to sleep and remain asleep. Lifestyle behaviors, hormonal changes, and health complaints, such as sleep apnea, restless leg syndrome, or pain, can also lead to disturbed sleep. This results in difficulties in concentration, memory retention, and problem-solving abilities, along with irritability, lethargy, and apathy. Studies reveal sleep disturbances and insomnia increase the risk of dementia and Alzheimer's disease. Research show that sleep and mental health/psychiatric disorders are also related. Poor sleep quality affects and creates havoc in every area of life. An adequate amount of sleep is essential for physical, mental, and emotional health and well-being.

When we can't sleep, the stress response is triggered, and the body releases cortisol, which suppresses the immune system. Another hormone that is released during sleep is the human growth hormone (HGH), which is known as the antiaging hormone. It aids in cellular repair, metabolism, and restoring the body. The majority of your HGH secretion is during sleep. Research shows that inadequate sleep can decrease the amount of HGH that the body secretes by the pituitary. HGH levels also naturally decline with age, so it's important to maintain higher levels. Good sleep hygiene and getting at least seven hours of sleep is necessary to increase these levels. Regular exercise will also boost HGH secretion.

As we age, our sleeping patterns can shift. We secrete less melatonin, the hormone that promotes sleep. According to the CDC's National Health and Nutrition Examination Survey, people over eighty years of age take more sleeping aids than those under forty. This may be due to other health problems that are interfering with sleep. It's good practice to develop proper sleeping habits early on to help prevent problems later in life. In the *New York Times* Sunday Review 2012 article, "The Case for Sleep Medicine," sleep scientist William Dement has argued, sleep is "the most important predictor of how long you will live—perhaps more important than smoking, exercise or high blood pressure."

It is vital to have a conducive bedtime ritual as part of your healthy lifestyle. Sleep affects every part of the body. Keep a regular sleep schedule by going to bed at the same time every night, even on the weekends. This will help maintain your circadian rhythms. A good night's sleep lets you begin your day refreshed, alert, and energized. Here are a few of the benefits:

- Improves reaction time and reflexes
- Improves concentration
- Supports cardiac health
- Reduces stress
- Reduces inflammation
- Helps maintain a healthy weight
- Improves immune function

Arranging Your Bedroom

A bedroom is an area for sleep and intimacy. Creating a bedroom that is conducive for rest and romance can help you sleep better and foster intimacy between you and your partner. Keep your bedroom dark and quiet with the room temperature on the colder side (70°F or below). Remove or unplug your electronics from the bedroom: TV, laptop, computer, smartphone, e-reader, and videogame console. The blue light emitted from these devices disrupts your circadian rhythm and suppresses melatonin, a hormone naturally produced by the pineal gland that produces drowsiness. Blue light signals the brain to wake up and stay awake. The National Sleep Foundation's 2014 Sleep in America poll revealed that "89% of adults and 75% of children have at least one electronic device in their bedrooms." Let your bedroom become an electronics- and distraction-free zone. It is your sacred sanctuary.

Plants in your bedroom can promote relaxation and be a natural sleep remedy. They can purify and improve air quality while giving off oxygen. Going to sleep surrounded by lavender, jasmine, or gardenia plants is quite a pleasant feeling. Aloe vera is another great choice, and it's easy to care for. They are also great to place around your house.

Preparing for Sleep

The following nighttime rituals are ones I personally use and share with my clients. Experiment with them. Pick and choose which ones you prefer. I hope they work as well for you as they have for my clients and me.

- ❖ Use the evening hours to release tension and relax. Spend precious time with loved ones. Phone a friend and have an uplifting conversation.

- ❖ Begin to let go of your day one hour before sleep. Choose your bedtime hour, so you have at least seven hours of sleep. Keep in mind what I mentioned earlier—that you want to be sleeping as much as possible between 10 p.m. and 2 a.m. when the body is repairing and restoring.

- Get in the habit of silencing your smartphone. Years ago, a friend once told me that a phone was a request, not a command. If you are concerned about missing an emergency call, some phones allow you to set the phone to alert you of calls coming from numbers you specify.

- Shut down your computer and turn off the TV. I recommend your last thoughts of the day not be the news or certain television shows that can either aggravate or frustrate you or create a feeling of sadness or worry.

- Dim the lights and create a relaxing ambiance. Play calming music and light some candles to help you wind down.

- Prepare an aromatherapy bath or take a warm shower. Imagine all the stress of the day being cleansed from the body and going down the drain.

- Give yourself a relaxing and grounding foot massage 15 minutes before sleep. It will move your energy downward from the head to the feet and calm the mind and induce sleep. Use warmed oils to create a soothing experience. You can use sesame oil for dry skin, coconut for sensitive or overheated skin, and sunflower oil for oily skin. Start at the ankle and move downward, massaging the entire foot including between the toes and the sole of the foot. You can also energize a sleep-inducing pressure point. To feel the point, curl your toes and look for the small depression beneath the ball of the foot and press lightly.

- Read an inspirational and uplifting book as you sip some chamomile or valerian tea or whatever noncaffeinated beverage is calming and satisfying to you.

- Diffuse or spray relaxing essential oils, such as lavender or bergamot, in your bedroom to relieve tension, lower heart rate, calm the nervous system, and reduce anxiety. To help you drift off to sleep, you can apply the fragrance on a piece of cloth and place the cloth inside your pillow case right before bed.

- Do not go to bed angry. If you cannot change the situation, surround your heart with loving, calm energy so you can sleep peacefully.

- When you get into bed, turn the clock away from you so you cannot see the time or the light from the clock.

Reflections on Your Day

End your day with uplifting thoughts by keeping a specific bedtime journal. Each night before you go to sleep, reflect on your day. Recall all of the things, no matter how big or small, that went well, even if it's as simple as finding an ideal parking spot or smiling at someone and they smile back. Take a few minutes to write them down as brief bullet points. Did you include helping another person or animal? As you continue to do this, you will approach each day looking more for the positive aspects of the day instead of focusing on negative thoughts or problems.

Total Body Relaxation Guided Imagery

This guided imagery can help you quiet the mind and promote deep relaxation. This is ideal for inducing sleep. You may even fall asleep before you reach the end. Wonderful! You can record this meditation for personal use and play it back to follow along. Speak slowly and let your voice soothe you. If you record it on your smartphone, silence the ringer and any alerts when you play it back.

Close the eyes and feel comfortably supported by the surface beneath you. Breathe in and out through the nose. Allow the breath to flow naturally and easily. Let the body breathe itself with its own natural rhythm.

Gently place your awareness on the left foot and notice if there is any tension there. Now with the power of intention, invite the left toes to release any tightness and relax. Let the breath flow naturally. Imagine there is healing light surrounding the toes. They are relaxed and soothed by this light. Feel this relaxation and light radiate throughout the left foot and up into the ankle. The left foot is completely comfortable and relaxed.

Gently shift your awareness to the right foot and notice if there is any tension there. Now invite the right toes to release any pressure and relax. Imagine there is healing light surrounding the right toes. They are relaxed and soothed by this light. Feel this relaxation and light radiate throughout the right foot and up into the ankle. The right foot is completely comfortable and relaxed. Both feet are enveloped inside soothing light.

Notice any tension you may be holding in the left calf and shin. Release and relax any tightness that may be there, as healing light enters this area. Let this sensation of relaxation and light spread down through the left ankle and foot. You cannot force the body to relax; you can only invite and allow the body to relax. Now notice any tension you may be holding in the right calf and shin. Invite these muscles to let go of any tightness. Allow healing light to enter this area as you teach the body to let go.

Now observe any tension you may be holding in the large muscles of the left thigh. Give these muscles permission to release tension and relax. As comforting light surrounds the left thigh, imagine the muscles loosening. As you let go more easily and deeply, observe any tension in the muscles of the right thigh. Release any tightness and relax these thigh muscles as light enters. Now invite this sensation of relaxation to deepen in both legs. Both legs are glowing in soothing light. You may have sensations of warmth, tingling, heaviness, or floating, which are all possible responses to deep relaxation.

Now bring your awareness to the muscles of the lower back and buttocks. Invite the lower back and buttocks to join in releasing and relaxing any unnecessary stress or tightness that may be there. Imagine light entering this area, encouraging the lower back muscles to broaden, flatten, and lengthen into deep relaxation.

Now be aware of any tightness you may be holding in the pelvis. Invite the pelvis to release. Relax the anal sphincter. Feel a deeper sense of relaxation and soothing light entering this area. Allow the sensations of relaxation deepen in the lower body, almost as if it was happening all by itself. When you relax any part of the body, the rest of the body relaxes as well.

Now encourage the abdomen and mid-back to release any stiffness, tension, or tightness. Allow these areas to join in the sense of relaxation. Imagine healing light relaxing the belly and mid-back. The abdomen is soft, open, and spacious. Feel the entire belly relaxing more deeply and comfortably.

Now loosen the muscles of the chest. Light radiates and relaxes the muscles between the ribs. Feel all the muscles on either side of the spine softly letting go, surrendering and immersed in light. Relax the muscles around and between the shoulder blades. The chest is enveloped in healing light. Allow the entire chest area to join in the sensation of relaxation and invite relaxation to deepen in every other part of you as well.

Now invite the sense of relaxation to expand to the muscles of the left shoulder. Let relaxation and light slowly flow down the left arm into the left wrist. Relaxation and healing light spread throughout the hand into the fingers. Let the fingers of the left hand glow in light and relax completely. You may feel pulsations in the fingertips as all the fingers of the left hand are comfortably relaxed.

Now invite the sense of relaxation to expand to the muscles of the right shoulder. Let relaxation and light slowly flow down the right arm into the right wrist. Relaxation and soothing light spread throughout the hand into the fingers. Let the fingers be aglow in light and relax completely.

Now gently bring your awareness to the area of the throat and relax any tightness or tension in the throat. Imagine soothing light creating more space inside the throat. Let this wave of relaxation and light seep into the muscles of the neck. Relax the chin and jaw, and let the teeth and lips part slightly, so there is no effort to even keep the lips closed. The tongue is thick and soft as relaxation spreads to the back of the tongue down into the throat. The sensation of relaxation moves in and around the mouth, across the teeth and lips. Relaxation encompasses the nose and expands, massaging the cheeks, the ears, and the temples. Soothing relief extends to the eyes and the eyebrows. Imagine there is more space between the eyebrows. Imagine the skin of the face and forehead is smooth. Let this relaxation radiate to the scalp. Invite the entire scalp to be loose and join in the sense of deep relaxation. The healing light moves up to surround and soothe the head. The whole body is flowing in deep, restful relaxation. Drifting. Calm. Peaceful, as you drift off to sleep.

YOUR TURN FOR SELF-DISCOVERY

A good night's sleep begins with a commitment to yourself. Reflect on your evening behaviors and habits. Are you supporting a well-deserved and relaxing end to your day?

Self-Inquiry Exercise: Before you begin, find a quiet place and allow 10 minutes for this exercise. Close the eyes and take a few deep breaths to focus your awareness. When you feel relaxed and centered, gently open the eyes. Spend a few moments thinking about what you learned in this chapter. In your journal, respond to the following prompts with your thoughts and insights:

- What are you willing to commit to when arranging your bedroom for a good night's sleep?

- Which rituals are you ready to begin adding to your life? Choose one to three rituals from the Preparing for Sleep list. After practicing these evening rituals for a few days, write about your experience in your journal. What did you notice about how you slept and your energy level the next day?

- Will you keep a journal for reflecting on your day? If so, after a few days to a week of keeping this journal, what did you notice? Share your inner wisdom.

- Did you do the Total Body Relaxation Guided Imagery? Comment on your experience.

In Closing

Sleep is vital for our health and well-being. Lifestyle behaviors and stress are the leading causes of disturbed sleep. As we age, health issues and medications can interrupt our sleep patterns. What are you willing to change to get a better night's sleep? It's never too late to develop good sleep habits. At first, it may feel uncomfortable or nearly impossible to do. Take it one step at a time. Here are some important points to remember:

- A soothing and relaxing bedroom promotes sleep.
- The hour before sleep is the time to wind down and prepare the body and mind to relax and drift off to sleep.
- Spending quality time during the evening hours with yourself and family is nurturing and bonding.
- Reflecting on the positive and uplifting moments of your day is a beautiful way to close the chapter of your day.
- Guided imagery is a useful technique to soothe you to sleep or help you get back to sleep.

In this chapter and the previous one, you learned how to live a health-promoting twenty-four-hour day in alignment with your biological rhythms. The next chapter will teach you how to manage life's stressors with proven coping strategies to help maintain that alignment and healthy balance.

CHAPTER 11

Coping Strategies

*"Every day brings a choice:
to practice stress or to practice peace."*
—DR. JOAN BORYSENKO

As we move about our day, stressors inevitably pop up. Caffeine, alcohol, drugs, and addictions like the internet are not effective approaches to deal with stress. We need proven and reliable techniques. Coping techniques help us be proactive in dealing with the perceived stressors in life rather than using avoidance or distraction as a means to handle stress. By being more aware of the issues, recognizing stressful scenarios, and identifying the origins of the anxiety and stress, we are able to see the stressors for what they really are and take action. The use of a repertoire of effective strategies and skills can decrease the stress response and lead to a change in behavior. Peacefully resolving the issues surrounding the situation allows us to think more clearly and to succeed and move forward.

In this chapter, I share with you approaches that can help you shed light on the challenges you face, discover the root cause, and take action to create peace of mind. Journaling, cognitive reframing, art therapy, and laughter and play therapy are all strategies I use with my clients and in personal practice. I hope you find them beneficial.

Journaling

The most effective coping skill is journaling. It has an emotional, cathartic effect and reduces the intensity of a stressor. It provides an avenue to release thoughts, feelings, and perceptions, including anger and fear. You can blow off steam and express anger safely and productively in a journal. Expressing your fears gets them out on the table, so you can see what you are afraid of and ask yourself, "Why am I afraid?"

Journaling is not a place to blame yourself or others or just write an account of a stressful or painful situation and go no further. It's about going deep within for insights and realizations. As you express yourself in writing, you are able to see the values, attitudes, and patterns of behavior in your life. Expressive writing increases self-awareness, self-expression, and self-reflection. It allows access to your inner knowledge and expression of the unconscious. You become more receptive to exploring positive and creative solutions and resolving the negative energy surrounding the stressors in your life.

In today's society, mental health issues are a significant concern. Journaling can help people better cope with anxiety and depression by processing, expressing, and working out their feelings, thoughts, and emotions. It allows us to clear our thoughts by getting the ideas out of our head and onto paper. Keeping pent-up, unresolved thoughts cluttering the mind can continue to build and jeopardize our mental health.

There are a variety of ways to journal. In Chapter 4, I shared using artistic expression as a way to gain insight into your life followed by writing your impressions of your drawing. This allowed the unconscious mind, the creative right side of the brain, to play and be revealed. Then the left logical and analytical brain brought it to a conscious level.

Another way to journal is what I call mental stressor dumping. Spend 5 minutes or longer unloading all of the stressful thoughts that are juggling around in your mind onto paper. Do this without stopping, like one continuous stream of thoughts. It's okay if your handwriting is sloppy. Write about what's bothering or frustrating you. Release the pressure cooker and clear the mind and heart of the stressors. Let it all go and create space in the mind. You may also notice your heart feels more spacious and lighter.

Journaling Exercise: Journaling is a path to self-discovery. Find a quiet area to write using paper and pen. Play soft music and/or light a naturally scented candle to get you in the mood. Make it a new habit to express yourself regularly. Devote 5 to 15 minutes a day to journaling. When you begin to write, date your entries. Do not censor or edit yourself. Keep writing and allow your stream of thoughts to flow without interruption. Be honest in your self-expression. If you get stuck and don't know what to write about, here are several suggestions to stimulate your thoughts. You can write about

- Your day
- Your ideas
- A memory
- What you are feeling in the moment
- What you are grateful for
- Your desires and dreams
- A favorite book, poem, or movie and why it's your favorite
- Your thoughts about what happened in the world today
- A question you have for yourself and your answer to it

Write about whatever comes to mind, even if it's about the weather. Just start writing. As you do, one thought will lead to another and to another and so on, and before you know it, you will have written a page or two. Once you get going, you may be surprised at how much you have to say about a topic. Afterward, you may want to reread and reflect on what you wrote. You may even come across some juicy nuggets or insights along the way. A journal can be a place to preserve your deepest thoughts, considerations, and memories.

Cognitive Reframing

When we change how we perceive something, the mind shifts. Reframing is the practice of taking responsibility for and turning our inner dialogue from negative, toxic thought patterns to positive, self-affirming perceptions. By stopping negative thoughts, accepting the situation as it is, and then considering a new way of thinking and replacing old thought patterns with positive affirmations that foster self-esteem, we are better able to see a positive side of the situation. Change starts by shifting the belief that alters or creates the feeling you are experiencing.

For every negative thought you have, there are positive alternatives and vice versa. How you perceive the moment will determine choice and the outcome that follows. A rainy day can be regarded as either challenging to get outdoor errands done or relaxing with time to attend to indoor projects, plus the plants are getting watered. Bumper-to-bumper traffic due to rubbernecking can be viewed as annoying with inept nosey drivers or as more alone time to listen to relaxing music or an audiobook. My early morning walks with my little fur baby can be seen as a tedious chore or, as I prefer, an opportunity to catch the sunrise and get some exercise and fresh air. Looking at things in a positive way reduces stress and promotes relaxation and peace of mind.

Keep in mind, too, that our perceptions are not always guided by facts. We can create expectations around misconceptions. This detaches us from the truth. We need to be aware of our thoughts and notice when we lean toward negative thinking. Then question if those negative thoughts are true by asking, "Where are my negative thoughts coming from? Am I seeing the full picture here? Is there another way of looking at this?" If your negative self-talk is still present, then replace it with a more positive twist.

Barry's Story

My client Barry shared an incident with me when he felt terrible and thoughtless. One of his coworkers, Sue, attended a meeting Barry was conducting. When he asked Sue a question, Sue didn't answer. Barry reprimanded her for not paying attention. Sue abruptly walked out of the meeting. Barry thought Sue was extremely rude and unprofessional for leaving and criticized her to the others in the meeting. After the meeting, Barry wanted to have a word with Sue, but he couldn't find her anywhere in the office. As he was again complaining, someone said to him, "How can you talk like that when Sue found out this morning that her best friend died in a car accident?"

Barry realized that he had jumped to the wrong conclusion and was embarrassed. His perceptions changed immediately. He now thought Sue was incredibly strong and loyal to the company to have come to the meeting in the first place. When Sue returned to the office, Barry apologized for criticizing her behind her back. Sue forgave him. This reframing was a learning experience for Barry, and he committed to not reacting negatively in the future about a situation before learning all the facts.

Art Therapy

In Chapter 4, I introduced you to art therapy through creative journaling. You expressed yourself through drawing and then interpreted that drawing. Art draws from imagination and personal skills to express an idea. Art therapy is a creative process that uses various materials and media to provide an avenue for nonverbal self-expression and communication. Research shows creating visual art is an effective coping strategy in reducing the physical, mental, and emotional outcomes of stress. It's useful when words are not enough or when it's hard to describe certain thoughts and feelings. Every image drawn or form produced with its details and omissions is significant and lends to individual meaning and self-interpretation.

You can express yourself through drawing, painting, sculpturing, creating a collage, or making jewelry. Creating a puppet or a stuffed animal or doll or making a mask are other ways to create art. Perhaps you prefer using clay, papier-mâché, or other natural materials. You can design a greeting card with a meaningful message. Photography and videography can also have therapeutic value and be viewed as art. Create a visual biography of your life. There are as many ideas as the mind can imagine. Need a little help? Perhaps enroll in an art class or get a coloring book. As you dip into your creative pool, it's important to know not to judge your finished art form. A perfect piece of art is not the goal. This is not a graded endeavor. It's a fun and cathartic release.

You can create art out of just about anything for any purpose. An artist and advocate friend of mine uses her art form to make a difference in the world. In her large and small paintings, she uses recycled materials and her creativity to tell a story and create environmental awareness. She uses art to deliver her message and forge ahead her movement for a litter-free planet.

Self-Inquiry Exercise: How often do you tap into your creative side? Spend a few minutes and review the various ways to express yourself using the art mediums suggested earlier or come up with your own forms. Use your imagination. The choices are endless. Now in your journal, list three creative activities you are open to exploring and willing to commit to making. Here's an example:

- Craft a collection book of my favorite quotes about nature. I will take my own photographs and include them.
- Connect with my inner child. Gather rocks, wash them, and then decorate with paint and/or significant words.

- Purchase a coloring book of mandalas, geometric designs symbolizing spirituality, and use my colored pencils.

Humor Therapy

Comic relief is useful to momentarily step outside your situation and regroup. You are able to release emotional stress and create a shift in awareness and embrace the paradox of life. Humor is a perception that helps in the healing process. It helps to increase pleasure and decrease pain and reduce anger and anxiety. Anger and laughter cannot coexist. The power of humor can allow you to feel more in control and joke about your situation. It can also create a diversion and interrupt the stress reaction and reduce the release of stress hormones.

Humor therapy has many benefits. Besides raising your mood and having fun, laughter boosts your immune function, increases oxygen in the blood, promotes relaxation, and releases endorphins, which are the body's natural painkillers. Find opportunities to laugh every day. Here are some ways to include humor in your daily life:

- Read and share jokes and cartoons.
- Don't take yourself so seriously.
- Connect with people who make you laugh.
- Dance to the oldies (i.e., Twist, Macarena, Robot, etc.)
- Watch comedy shows.
- Create a comedy movie night at home.
- Consciously smile at people.
- Find the humor in serious or intense situations.
- Plan a fun and interactive family game night.
- Be silly and engage in playful activities and humorous skits.

- Create a backyard, outdoor, or indoor obstacle race course.
- Find something to laugh about before going to sleep.
- Remember what it was like to have fun and play as a child. What were you doing? Consider doing that now.

YOUR TURN FOR SELF-DISCOVERY

The stressors in life don't change, but your ability and the way you handle stress can change. In this chapter, you learned some techniques to cope with stress and its emotions. Now it's your turn to commit to yourself.

Self-Inquiry Exercise: Before you begin, find a quiet place and allow 10 to 15 minutes for this exercise. Close the eyes and take a few deep breaths to focus your awareness. When you feel relaxed and centered, gently open the eyes and begin. In your journal, describe how you will incorporate each of the four coping strategies—journaling, cognitive reframing, art therapy, and humor therapy—into your life. Be specific and choose one way for each. Also, note how each of these strategies will be helpful in your life and what you noticed after experiencing each approach. Here's an example of how this might look:

Journaling: Mental stressor dumping

How it will be helpful: It will allow me to release the negative thoughts that are cluttering my mind.

What I noticed: I felt lighter and calmer afterward.

Cognitive Reframing: Beginning to replace negative thoughts with positive ones

How it will be helpful: I'll consider the glass half full instead of half empty.

What I noticed: It was difficult at first to catch all the negative thoughts, but I started to get the hang of it and actually felt more positive about things in general.

Art Therapy: Get a coloring book of mandalas

How it will be helpful: Creating a colorful picture design will be fun and relaxing.

What I noticed: I enjoyed the downtime. I was amazed and proud of the beautiful piece of artwork I made. The colors expressed exactly how I was feeling.

Humor Therapy: Watch a comedy

How it will be helpful: It will get me to laugh, which will be a welcome relief.

What I noticed: I definitely felt more relaxed afterward, and I enjoyed thinking about the movie instead of tomorrow's to-do list.

In Closing

Coping strategies are effective in reducing stress by managing and resolving the stressors in your life. Discovering and dealing with the root cause of the challenges we face and not sidestepping them are crucial factors. These are the key points to remember:

- One of the most effective coping skills is journaling. It's about clearing your head and expressing yourself to realize and reduce the root causes of stress. It's a soul-searching strategy that helps you learn more about yourself, your values, and your behaviors, which can lead to solutions for a better life.

- Reframing is a way to alter your perceived stressors, thereby reducing the fight/flight/freeze response. Replacing negative thought patterns and self-talk with more positive statements changes how you look at a situation or something in particular. These shifts create learning experiences.

- Art therapy uses art forms and nonverbal ways to express yourself when words are not enough. The purpose is to help you process your emotions in a healthy way; it isn't about creating a polished piece of artwork for display.

- Humor therapy is a fun and proven skill to cope with stress. Adopt this motto: "Laughter and play, every day."

Half of holistic stress management is becoming skilled in coping strategies such as the ones you learned in this chapter. The other half is learning how to relax. Next, we will explore specific relaxation techniques to help you reduce the symptoms of stress.

CHAPTER 12

Your Personal Relaxation Plan

"The time to relax is when you don't have time for it."
—SYDNEY HARRIS

When was the last time you were really deeply relaxed with no stress or scattered thoughts? Do you know how to train the body to relax? In my practice, I realized that many people do not know how to relax or know how deep relaxation feels. When I've asked clients what they do to relax, these are some of the answers: go out to dinner, watch TV, go to the movies, play a video game, hang out with friends, and go on vacation. These activities are more distracting than relaxing. For example, watching TV does not allow the body to go into deep relaxation because it is mentally stimulating and, depending on what you are viewing, can be stressful. Going out somewhere is activating the body, and there is a chance of having the stress response triggered. So, let's look at true relaxation techniques now so that you can start putting them into practice.

Why We Need Relaxation Techniques

The purpose of relaxation is to interrupt the stress response, support the immune system, and bring the mind and body back to a place of balance, or homeostasis. Relaxation techniques and practices inhibit the sympathetic nervous system's release of stress hormones that increase blood pressure and heart and breathing rates. When the parasympathetic nervous system is activated, it counteracts the stress response and brings the body back into harmonious balance. Cortisol levels are lowered, heart and breathing rates slow down, and blood pressure is reduced. Muscle relaxation is induced, and your energy is replenished. The production of oxytocin, which is referred to as the love hormone, increases to help maintain homeostasis. The body is able to rest and repair itself while promoting a sense of inner peace and well-being.

For all of these reasons, we need to include relaxation techniques in our daily routine. Using the skills, procedures, and practices regularly is beneficial in creating the relaxation response. They are most effective when combined with coping strategies, such as the ones you learned about in the previous chapter. Relaxation techniques alleviate the symptoms of stress, whereas coping strategies clear the causes. The goals are to achieve and support increased self-awareness, positive self-esteem, inner peace, and well-being.

There many ways to enter into deep relaxation. The best techniques to put into your relaxation plan are the ones you are willing to do and commit to practice. I've already discussed meditation as an ideal way to de-stress, so I'm going to focus on a few different approaches that allow you to let go, release tension, and restore balance.

Physical Activity

Physical activities like yoga, qigong, tai chi, and walking in nature are relaxation practices that connect mind, body, and spirit. They invite you to draw your awareness inward and align the breath and body as one flowing energy. Yoga helps lower blood pressure and heart rate, strengthen muscles, increase flexibility, and improve posture. Qigong and tai chi are forms of energy work that can be described as moving meditation. They use slow movements to improve body strength, flexibility, and balance. Strolling in nature can be an insightful and mindful walking meditation experience. These are just a few physical activity examples to consider.

Some people are drawn to more vigorous physical activity to release pent-up physical tension, let off steam, relax the mind and body, and *get in the zone*. Aerobic exercise like running, swimming, cycling, tennis, fast walking, stairclimbing, and fitness classes creates a stress-relieving cardiovascular workout. As you engage your large muscles, your breathing and heart rate increase, delivering more oxygen to the body for optimal functioning. Working out helps reduce anxiety, clear the mind of mental clutter, alleviate mild depression, and promote relaxation.

When the body feels more alert and energized, we have a better outlook on life. All types of exercise release endorphins, the natural painkiller and mood-elevating hormones released by the body. It's responsible for the *runners' high*, the euphoric feeling a person experiences after running. This elated feeling is combined with a sense of relaxation. Daily physical activity is beneficial regardless of age, ability, or weight, so find what works for you, and stick with it.

Important Note

When it comes to physical activity and the next technique, conscious breathing, always check with your health-care provider about what is appropriate for you. If you have lung or heart conditions, such as shortness of breath, asthma, or hypertension, consult your health-care provider before doing any breathing practices. Anyone with cardiac problems should not hold their breath for extended periods. While doing a breathing technique, if you feel dizzy or light-headed, stop the practice and resume regular breathing.

The Art of Conscious Breathing

Have you ever noticed yourself holding your breath when you feel tense, anxious or stressed? Are you aware of how you breathe? Do you breathe from the chest or the belly? Do you find yourself yawning frequently? Proper conscious breathing is the key to releasing stress and anxiety, relaxing, and promoting health. I will teach you three simple yet powerful breathing practices you can use every day.

When we are breathing correctly, we usually breathe between twelve and sixteen times per minute. Relaxed breathing is about eight to twelve breaths per minute. Deep meditative breathing, an advanced practice, is slow and controlled breathing between one and four times per minute. When we feel anxious or upset, the breath rate increases. When the mind is calm and quiet, the breath rate slows down. To master the mind, we must master the breath.

Belly Breathing

More than half of my clients have been surprised that they needed to learn how to breathe again. I explained how the breathing process works. It's essential that we activate the diaphragm muscle and lungs fully to supply the body with sufficient oxygen, so the body's tissues and vital organs receive adequate nourishment. The diaphragm is the dome-shaped muscle that is located at the base of the lungs and above the stomach. When we breathe in, the abdominal muscles relax and the diaphragm contracts downward, pulling air into the lungs while moving the abdominal organs out of the way. As you breathe out, the diaphragm relaxes, and the abdominal muscles contract, pushing the air up and out of the lungs. These movements strengthen the diaphragm and abdominal muscles. This is called diaphragmatic breathing or belly breathing. It triggers the relaxation response, releases muscular tension, calms the nervous system, and increases energy.

The biggest cause of improper breathing is our posture and stress. When we slouch at our desk or while sitting on the couch, our diaphragm cannot contract and relax. The lungs are not able to expand, so we don't take as much air into the lungs or completely empty the lungs. This creates shallow chest breathing. The breathing rate can increase in an attempt to supply more oxygen to the body. Oxygen deficiency can lead to fatigue, mental challenges, anxiety, and chronic stress issues. However, it's never too late to learn how to breathe!

The Practice: Find a quiet place to practice this technique. When you feel relaxed and centered, begin. You may find it easier to first do this breathing practice lying down with the knees bent and head and neck well supported. Place one hand on the chest to help you be aware of keeping the chest still. Place the other hand on the belly above the navel so you can feel the movement of the diaphragm and the rise and fall of the abdomen.

- Breathe in slowly and gently through the nose, so the air passes through the cilia, the tiny hairs inside the nose that clean the air. Slowly breathe out through the nose.

- As you breathe in slowly, let the air fill the belly, as you feel the belly rise under the hand. Do not push the abdominal muscles outward making the belly bulge. The hand over the chest remains somewhat motionless.

- As you breathe out, follow the out breath to the end, as you slowly draw the abdominal muscles inward. Notice the momentary pause before you breathe in again. Let the breath complete itself.

- When you breathe in again, the in breath will be naturally fuller, expanding the lungs with oxygen. Keep the breath flow smooth and even.

- There are three parts to this breath: the exhale, pause, and the inhale.

- Relax and let the breath deepen, and notice your awareness drifting inward.

- Continue belly breathing for 5 minutes.

❖ When you finish, observe any changes or sensations you may be feeling.

Seated variation: Find a quiet place to practice this technique. When you feel relaxed and centered, begin. You may find it easier to first do this breathing practice lying down with the knees bent and head and neck well supported. Place one hand on the chest to help you be aware of keeping the chest still. Place the other hand on the belly above the navel so you can feel the movement of the diaphragm and the rise and fall of the abdomen.

I suggest that you practice this breathing exercise for 5 minutes three times a day. If you like, you can schedule it to coincide before your meals. In this way, the body will be relaxed to aid in digestion. Then increase the time until it becomes second nature to you. As with any type of physical exercise, practice is required. Start slowly and continue to strengthen the diaphragm and expand the lungs.

Bumblebee Breath

A simple breathing practice is called bhramari, also known as the bumblebee breath. Besides producing deep relaxation as the breathing rate naturally slows down, it helps reduce anxiety and anger and calms the mind. It has a soothing effect on the nervous system. You can also use this breathing practice lying down to fall asleep.

The Practice (simple version): Find a quiet place to practice this technique. Sit up straight either in a chair or cross-legged on the floor. Drop the shoulders and relax the jaw. When you feel relaxed and centered, begin.

❖ Breathe in and out through the nose.

❖ Now with the mouth closed, exhale making a soft and steady *mmm* sound like a bumblebee. Choose a lower pitch tone that is comfortable to hum.

- Imagine you are saying *mmm* continuously as you breathe out.

- Keeping the humming sound smooth and even all the way to the end of the out breath. Let the sound taper off without straining. Allow the breath to complete itself as you notice the momentary pause before you breathe in again through the nose.

- Continue with the humming sound on the exhale. Let the soothing sound flow with the breath. Feel the sound vibrating within and relaxing any tightness or tension or releasing impurities from the body.

- Practice this for 10 to 15 breath cycles. One cycle is one complete inhalation and exhalation.

Do this practice on an empty stomach. Morning is ideal, right before meditation. Do not strain as you produce the sound. Stop whenever you feel the need. If you get dizzy, stop and return to regular breathing. You may not be used to receiving so much oxygen. You can practice this when you feel stressed or tired.

Do not use this technique while driving a vehicle. I like to use the bumblebee breath when I come to a three-minute traffic light. It helps me stay balanced and chilled out as I go through my day. I also do three or four bhramari breath cycles before a business meeting to be focused and clear. Sometimes I use it to center myself before my afternoon meditation, especially if I feel too energized.

Alternate Nostril Breathing

Nadi shodhana, or alternate nostril breathing, is a yoga breathing technique that purifies (shodhana) or cleanses the subtle energy channels (nadis). It regulates the flow of oxygen through the nasal passageways. According to Ayurveda, it harmonizes and balances the two hemispheres of the brain, activates the parasympathetic (relaxed) nervous system, and improves lung functioning. It helps release anxiety, calm the mind, and bring you back to feeling centered.

The Practice: Find a quiet place to practice this technique. Before your start, blow your nose. Then sit up tall, either in a chair or cross-legged on the floor. Relax the shoulders and the jaw. When you feel relaxed and centered, begin.

- Relax the left hand in your lap or on your thigh. Lift the right hand and gently place the pointer finger on the bridge of the nose. Position the thumb next to the right nostril and the middle and ring finger next to the left nostril.
- Close the eyes. Breathe in deeply through both nostrils.
- As you exhale, close the right nostril with the thumb, so you are breathing through the left nostril.
- Keeping the right nostril closed, gently inhale through the left nostril slowly and gradually.
- Close the left nostril with the middle and ring fingers, release the thumb, and exhale slowly and completely through the right nostril. Do not strain.
- Inhale through the right nostril.
- Close the right nostril and open and exhale through the left nostril.
- This is one round, or breath cycle.
- Practice this for 5 to 10 rounds. Keep the inhalations and exhalations smooth and at the same tempo and length. As with belly breathing, follow the out breath to the end. To complete, return to breathing through both nostrils.

I've used alternate nostril breathing when I want to be clear and focused, like to write this book or to get centered before meditation. It can help to calm the monkey mind so you can let go and drift off to get a good night's sleep. If you are feeling a little stuffy or you have challenges with allergies, this technique can help clear your nasal passageways.

Guided Imagery

In Chapter 10, you received the Total Body Relaxation Guided Imagery script to help you fall asleep. Guided imagery, likened to daydreaming, uses the flow of thoughts from the imagination and unconscious mind for relaxation and healing. You are in complete control at all times. Guided imagery can influence the major regulatory systems of the body and enhance insight and self-awareness. The Sacred Forest is a guided imagery meditation to help you feel calm and relaxed with a sense of inner peace. You can use this imagery when you need to shift to a more positive mood or you need to reduce tension or discomfort in the body and promote healing. It's an ideal stress-management tool to better cope with challenges and promote a sense of harmony. It can help transport you to a place where you feel more spiritually connected and insightful.

> ### Sacred Forest Guided Imagery Meditation
>
> You can record this meditation for personal use and play it back to follow along. Speak slowly and let your voice soothe you. If you record it on your smartphone, silence the ringer and any alerts when you play it back. Find a quiet place to practice this meditation. When you feel relaxed and centered, begin.
>
> *As you gently close the eyes, be aware of the surface beneath you. Feel the heels of the feet connecting with the surface . . . the hips . . . the upper back . . . the head. Let the body be comfortably supported by this surface . . . grounded . . . safe.*
>
> *Now place your attention on the abdomen. As you breathe in and out through the nose, observe the rise and fall of the*

belly. Relax the jaw, letting the lips and teeth part slightly. Now as you enjoy four deep breaths, invite yourself to breathe in relaxation and breathe out any tension or tightness. Invite the body to relax and let go, as you remain awake and alert.

Imagine you are walking along a path leading into a forest in the early morning hours on a clear spring day. The path is a carpet of fallen leaves and crackling twigs beneath your feet. The air is moist and crisp with a refreshing fragrance. As you look around, you become aware of the various shades of colors that decorate this forest. You notice the tall majestic trees beckoning and reaching toward the brilliant blue sky that is painted with a few white puffy clouds passing by. You walk over and touch one of the trees. Your fingers and palms caress and feel the rough and smooth textures. With your arms, you hug the tree and become aware of the tree's coolness, its strength, and its stability. Feel nurtured, safe, and empowered in this natural environment.

As you continue down a lush vegetative path, you notice a blueberry bush full of succulent, juicy berries. As you look closer, you observe dewdrops gracefully positioned on the rough surface of the leaves. The dewdrops glisten and sparkle with the morning rays. You smile, looking at the reflection in the dewdrop. You pick one of the blueberries and let your fingers gently explore its shape and texture. You hold it up to your lips and inhale its subtle fragrance. As you bite into it, you savor its refreshing sweet or sour taste.

Now your attention is drawn to the sounds of small creatures scurrying about in all directions. Some are gathering food. Others appear playful. In the distance, you notice sunlight peering through the treetops, traveling as beams of radiant light down to the earth. As you continue to move toward this light, you come to a small body of tranquil water. You remove your shoes to cross the calm pond. Flat stepping-stones lead the way to the other side. You are as happy as a child as you walk, skip, and leap from stone to stone, occasionally splashing water with your toes. Feel the cool, watery rocks supporting you to the other side.

As you reach the other side, your bare feet touch and absorb the energy of the Earth. You feel deeply grounded and connected. Look around and see the beams of light illuminating a clearing. You sense this place to be one of great healing. As you move closer, you know that it is a sacred gathering place. Walking barefoot you move closer and become aware of places to sit that are made out of smooth tree trunks. You choose a spot to recline, one with thick green moss covering its surface like a soft blanket. Lie comfortably on your back and feel the softness. Breathe in the breath and vitality of the forest, alive with energy. Allow this harmonious relationship to center and relax you.

A gentle breeze carries the soothing sounds of birds nestled high above in the trees. Feel the tension melt away as their songs caress and comfort you. Feel the warmth of the sun's rays envelope you, embrace you, and radiate around and within you. Look up beyond the treetops and notice the vastness, the massiveness of the open sky. Now absorb the energy of this magical place. And simply let go.

Now enjoy a gentle deep breath as you come back to this time and place. Listen to the sounds around you. Feel the surface beneath you. Wiggle the toes and fingers. Observe the state of mind and body at this moment. Slowly open the eyes. Bring this sense of appreciation and wholeness with you throughout your day, knowing that you can return to this place whenever you wish.

YOUR TURN FOR SELF-DISCOVERY

You learned techniques to reduce the effects and symptoms of stress from the mental, emotional, and physical bodies. Now it's time to evaluate the effects of relaxation and consciously consider the benefits you experienced. Taking note of how you benefited will increase your willingness to practice regularly.

Self-Inquiry Exercise: Before you begin, find a quiet place and allow 10 to 15 minutes for this exercise. Close the eyes and take a few deep breaths to focus your awareness. When you feel relaxed and centered, gently open the eyes and begin. In your journal, respond to the following prompts with your thoughts and insights:

- Which physical activity for relaxation (yoga, qigong, tai chi, walking in nature, or similar type of activity) will you commit to and why?

- After you practice each of the breathing techniques, note any changes in your breathing and your state of mind and body. What did you notice? Include comments for each type of breathing exercise.

- Describe your experience and insights following the Sacred Forest Guided Imagery Meditation.

In Closing

Teaching the body how to relax helps bring the body and mind back into balance. The ideal practices to use are the ones you will do daily. If you start with learning to belly breathe and add just one other relaxation technique, you will begin to notice a shift in your response to life's stressors. Breathing properly is essential to health and wellness. It is an affordable and readily available way to relax anywhere, anytime.

Listening to a guided imagery journey invites you to just *be* and not have to physically do anything.

Congratulations on completing Part Three! You know how to

- Practice a morning ritual so you can begin your day centered and focused.

- Eat with more awareness and in a way that supports wellness.

- Follow an evening ritual to prepare for a better night's sleep.

- Choose to utilize effective coping strategies when faced with challenges.

- Set aside time daily to nurture your well-being with relaxation techniques.

Well done! You're moving forward.

PART FOUR

Emotional Healing, Meaningful Relationships

"Your task is not to seek for love, but merely to seek and find all the barriers within yourself that you have built against it."

—RUMI

Throughout a day, you experience a myriad of thoughts and emotions that affect the body and how you interact with the world around you. With every thought you have, the body responds. This is the premise of the mind-body connection. As the mind thinks, the body creates. If you are experiencing happy thoughts, the body may feel light and full of energy and you are socially outgoing. On the other hand, if you are having feelings of deep sadness, the body may feel sluggish and heavy and you want to be left alone. As we change our thought patterns, the body and mind respond accordingly.

We experience life through our thoughts. Our feelings give meaning to our thoughts in the moment. When we bring the past or future into the present moment, we can open ourselves to unresolved anger, fear, pain, and hurt. Emotional pain stems from unresolved emotional issues you are having with yourself or others at that moment. If you are waiting for situations in your life to change to be happy, you will be waiting for a long time. Looking inward is where resolution and lasting change begins. Are you ready to let go of suffering? Do you want to heal your emotions and be free? Are you ready for fulfilling relationships?

As you continue your journey in Part Four, you will learn how to unleash emotional stress and know how to manage and release anger, and fear. You will explore how to release self-sabotaging thoughts and cultivate empowering beliefs. Learn to use your inner resources to build resilience. I will guide you in knowing how to set healthy boundaries and say *yes* to you. Discover what it takes for a healthy relationship with yourself and others.

CHAPTER 13

The Positive Side of Anger

"Sloth, apathy, and despair are the enemy.
Anger is not. Anger is our friend. Not a nice friend.
Not a gentle friend. But a very, very loyal friend."

—JULIA CAMERON

Do you find being calm a challenge? Do you ever feel like your anger is out of control? Anger is a healthy survival emotion. Expressing anger is important for mental health. We learn how to process negative emotions as they are happening, diffuse anger, and settle conflicts. However, prolonged and unresolved anger, hostility, cynicism, rage, and guilt can create a continuous stress loop and health issues. Anger arises when we expect a certain turnout of events and that expectation is not met. Depression and its many forms can surface. It's been said that depression is anger turned inward toward yourself. According to the Center for Disease Control, by 2014, about one in every eight Americans over the age of twelve reported recent use of antidepressants. One of America's largest pharmacies, Express Scripts, reported a 15% increase in antidepressant use from 2015–2019.

The cruxes of every symptom, stress, and disease are emotions and memories that are buried in our subconscious mind. This is the elephant in the room. Our trapped emotions are the source of everything that upsets us. Anger and its many faces can surface when we come up against an unmet expectation or remember a previous hurt or pain that was not resolved. We tend to hold on to the anger to protect us from that situation if it happens again. These past memories are in our imagination. Our pain and hurt come from our interpretation of these memories. We choose to give power to our memories.

It's important to understand how to let go of negative emotions and restore them with positive thoughts, feelings, and emotions. Just as anger is a healthy emotion, both positive and negative emotions are essential for mental health. Our goal is not to experience only positivity. Anger can be helpful. Some negativity can help us shift our awareness to focus on being more supportive and creative in our choices. Life is a balance between positivity and negativity.

Expressing Anger

We've all experienced the dark side of anger. I was introduced to the concept of mismanaged anger categorized into four distinct styles by Dr. Brian Luke Seaward, author of *Managing Stress: Principles and Strategies for Health and Well-Being*. In his lectures, he shared the work of Dr. Neil Clark Warner, author of *Make Anger Your Ally*. Dr. Warren describes the four styles of handling anger as somatizers, self-punishers, exploders, and underhanders. The different behaviors displayed in each of these styles are all control dramas used to express anger. Be aware of these ineffective ways to handle anger when they surface. This allows your focus to shift to modifying negative behavior patterns.

Exploders hold in their anger until they verbally and/or physically explode with hostile aggression. They may hold back their feelings of anger toward the one they are angry with and then hurl that anger onto innocent targets who had nothing to do with the initial episode. To gain control over others, they display such bullying behaviors as cursing, verbal intimidation, physical abuse, slamming doors, throwing objects, hitting things or people, and road rage.

Somatizers suppress, bottle up, and swallow their feelings out of fear of rejection and not being liked. They play the martyr role. The anger is directed back inward, and the body pays the price. The body can show symptoms like migraines and tension headaches, TMJ, arthritis, chest pains, and gastrointestinal problems.

Self-punishers are unwilling to grant themselves an appropriate way to express and vent anger. They are often depressed. The frustration and guilt they feel for getting angry turns into belittling and punishing themselves. They can engage in excessive, undesirable behaviors such as overeating, anorexia, bulimia, self-mutilation, drinking too much, and drug use.

Underhanders impose passive-aggressive behavior on their targeted individuals. They want revenge and direct their anger directly at the person involved usually in socially acceptable ways. They are sly in their approach and may wait until a person leaves the room before talking negatively about them to others. This backstabbing behavior is coupled with sarcasm, insinuations, and guilt, and often combined with harsh humor.

Adam's Story

My client Adam lost his young son to a drunk driver. The "exploder" in him mishandled the anger and consumed him for over a year, to the point that friends and family felt uncomfortable around him. After practicing effective ways to deal with anger, he had a major turning point. His life condition shifted when he took the energy of that anger and transformed it with his dedication and creativity to stand up and make a difference. He created support groups together with his wife to help parents cope with the loss of a child to a drunk driver. To increase awareness of the importance to not drink and drive, he shares his story with local schools and church groups. His mission gives him the strength and resilience to keep going.

We all display mismanaged anger styles at times. Somatizers and self-punishers direct their anger at themselves. Exploder and underhanders direct their anger at others. As you review the descriptions, notice which style you identify with most when you are not managing your anger well. Perhaps you have characteristics and behaviors from another category as well. That's all right. It's also possible to display a combination of all of them, using different styles with different situations or people. Do not judge yourself based on your mismanaged anger style or styles. Be honest with yourself. Only when you know your style can you learn to deal with it and make new choices, and be free from any unwanted behaviors.

8 Ways to Manage Anger

Knowing your anger style is helpful because you can start to monitor and manage it. You cannot change what you don't know. It's important to adopt new habits to dissolve anger. The following are eight anger management guidelines you can use to befriend anger, allow it to be constructive, and make it work for you.

1. **Avoid anger triggers.** Lessen your exposure to situations that trigger your anger. There is a saying, "Every upset is a setup." If you know something will upset you, avoid it. Notice your thoughts surrounding your perceived stressors and realize outside stressors do not have to affect your inner world. We can shift our awareness to realize the difference between living from the outside in to manifesting our life from the inside out. When we view the outside world as the cause of our suffering, we succumb to the many triggers to set off a feeling of anger. With outside-in living, we see the things "out there" as the cause of much unhappiness and conflict. Turning our attention inward, living from the inside out, we choose to not let those outside stressors affect us and trigger anger. We recognize anger, and how we respond to it is a choice.

2. **Clear the emotional impact.** To help release some of the effects of anger that impact the body, we use our awareness, the breath, and our intentions in a three-step process. You can use this technique whenever anger or negative emotion surface:

    ❖ **Step one:** Identify the unsettling emotion you are experiencing and take responsibility for it. It's no one else's emotion. Accept that you are feeling angry. You choose your thoughts and how you wish to think and feel in every moment.

    ❖ **Step two:** Close the eyes and turn your attention inward. Find where you are feeling that emotion in the body. Notice the sensations you are feeling. Allow your attention to embrace what you feel. Now imagine you are breathing into that part of the body. Have the intention of sending the breath to relax and soften that area. Hear the message the emotion is carrying. As you continue to envision the area expanding with the breath, feel the body shift. The charge of that emotion no longer has power over you. Notice the mind is also calming down. Once the anger dissipates, open the eyes.

    ❖ **Step three:** To help you get clear and gain insight, express the emotion either through journaling or with a support person who knows how to be a sounding board or conscious listener. As you release the thoughts surrounding anger, you are more open to letting go of the anger in a positive, creative, and productive way.

3. **Release the anger.** It's helpful to vent anger in the moment when it arises instead of waiting for it to build up. Release the anger from the physical body through some form of activity. Perhaps running, talking a brisk walk, or hitting tennis or golf balls. Humor is a way to lighten up the intensity of the situation. Art therapy, as I mentioned in Chapter 11, is another place you can release your anger through self-expression. Being a classical pianist, I like to

play pieces that allow me to physically release anger while I get to listen to beautiful music, too. Sometimes, releasing anger in this way gets my creative juices flowing, and I start composing music. Expressing creativity allows you to be in the present moment where change happens.

4. **Let go of expectations.** When we have our heart set on something, we get upset if it doesn't come to fruition. Expectations are thoughts we project into the future. To be clear, this is not about goal setting. When we expect something, we spend time trying to convince others to make that belief happen. This goes nowhere. We do not control our future thoughts because we don't know what we will be thinking about next. When we have no expectations, we accept things as they are and respond in the moment.

5. **Create your support team.** Everyone experiences the stress of hardships. At times, we need emotional and spiritual support from family, friends, and even our pets when it comes to dealing with anger. For some, asking for help is difficult. Feelings of inadequacy or embarrassment may come up. Express yourself to the people you know will be open to hearing your truth and with whom you can be your authentic self. Members of your support team act as sounding boards, so you can express your insights and get honest feedback. They may offer possible new insights or ideas for your contemplation. Receiving support can reduce stress and anger and help alleviate anxiety and depression.

6. **Be open to different realities.** People have different viewpoints and separate realities. Every person has their own way of thinking that determines their individual reality. It's not about being right or wrong. When we shift our perceptions in knowing this, we can be open to a greater understanding and acceptance of others. (See Fran's Story on the following page for an example of this.)

7. **Calm down.** When you feel threatened or angry, become aware of the breath. Do not hold the breath or breathe shallow, which can increase the anger. Allow the breath to relax you. Use the belly breath or bumblebee breath you learned in Chapter 12 to relax.

8. **Cool down.** Another useful breathing technique is called sitkari, or cooling breath. It helps to cool the body to decrease the heated, fiery emotion of anger in the body. It will also activate the parasympathetic nervous system to lessen the effects of stress. Here's how to practice the cooling breath:

   - Sit up straight either in a chair or cross-legged on the floor.
   - Purse your lips to make a tiny round opening. Breathe in slowly through this opening, like breathing in through a straw. The tongue is pressing against the back of the bottom teeth. Feel the coolness of the air enter and pass over the tongue.
   - Then close the mouth and breathe out through the nose. Follow the out breath to the end.
   - Allow the breath to fill the belly as you inhale completely through pursed lips.
   - Fully exhale as you breathe out through the mouth.
   - Continue breathing this way for 1 to 3 minutes. If you get dizzy or light-headed, stop and return to regular breathing.

Fran's Story

Fran found it difficult to politely remove herself from conversations that got her blood boiling, especially those with her close friend. I asked her why she insisted on staying in a situation that only resulted in her getting upset and angry time and time again. She said that they were longtime friends, and she couldn't just get up and leave her group of friends. "Besides, what's wrong with a good debate?" was her retort.

Once Fran understood the implications of separate realities (that is, that each person has a particular way of viewing things), she did not participate in trying to be right or try to convince others of her point of view. She started to see how criticizing others was going nowhere, so she stopped. As time went along, she found the others in the group followed her lead. Heated debates no longer cornered the conversation. The friends all became more in tune with each other.

YOUR TURN FOR SELF-DISCOVERY

No one is immune to feeling frustrated and angry from time to time. How you express anger is a learned behavior, and it is entirely in your control to develop a new behavior. It's vital to know your mishandled anger style and discover new behaviors that support a positive outlet.

Self-Inquiry Exercise: Before you begin, find a quiet place and allow 10 to 15 minutes for this exercise. Close the eyes and take a few deep breaths to focus your awareness. When you feel relaxed and centered, gently open the eyes. In your journal, respond to the following prompts with your thoughts and insights:

- What is your main mismanaged anger style?
- How many times a day do you feel anger and frustration? Recall the past twenty-four hours and reflect on your daily activities, conversations, or watching the media.
- List three ways you have been reducing anger and frustration (e.g., breathe, walk away, find humor in the situation).

❖ Name three people you consider to be part of your support system and why.

Drawing from the 8 Ways to Manage Anger on pages 138–141, create your personal anger action plan. Share the steps you commit to following when your anger is triggered. Notice which top-three approaches are your most favorite. Write your plan in your journal. Here's an example of an Anger Action Plan to get you started.

Anger Action Plan

Situation: Heated arguments during family gatherings
Anger styles: Somatizer and underhander
Plan:

❖ Accept that arguments are inevitable and not to expect this time to be any different. I'm tired of getting my hopes up and feeling irritable and disappointed later.

❖ Recognize that different family members have different points of view. Stay out of getting caught in the middle of verbal arguments.

❖ Remember to avoid talking about anything political. This is the topic that sparks family tempers.

❖ Refrain from trying to convince others of another way of seeing something or defending another's viewpoint. This wastes my energy and gets me nowhere.

❖ Stop speaking badly about another family member in their absence.

❖ Recognize when I am experiencing anger and not suppress it. Focus on my breathing to keep me relaxed and calm.

- Excuse myself from heated discussions and take a walk with my cousin who is my emotional ally and comic relief.
- Find the levity in the situation. Watch the family dynamics as a humorous play.

In Closing

Anger can be a healthy survival emotion when handled effectively. It commands us to respond to a situation and find safe solutions. Anger can motivate, empower, and protect us. It begins in our thoughts around our past, present, and projected hurts. When we do not resolve the issues and relieve our suffering, our remembered pain turns inward and becomes anger. Our perceived stressors can trigger our fight/flight/freeze response, resulting in irritability, frustration, and its other related emotions. Here are some points to remember:

- It's important to know your mismanaged anger style so that you can recognize the patterns and behaviors and transform them into a positive outcome.
- Release the emotional charge of stress and anxiety as it is happening to avoid bottling it up and exploding later.
- Develop ways to release and manage anger.
- Create your personal anger management plan. Practice the steps, so they become a natural behavioral response to relieving anger. Use it creatively to your benefit.

In the next chapter, I'll guide you in the process of releasing fear, which is another stress emotion. We will also take a deeper look at how limiting beliefs hold you back from the life you deserve.

CHAPTER 14

Releasing Fear-Based Beliefs

"Limits, like fear, is often an illusion."
—MICHAEL JORDAN

Like anger, fear is a healthy survival mechanism that we can use to our benefit. Fear helps us identify what is and is not a threat. Our fears protect us by cautioning us to be more alert and focused on potential danger. Many fears are caused by events that trigger the fight/flight/freeze response. When we feel threatened, fear can prompt us to run away and escape the danger, defend ourselves, or freeze in place like a deer in the headlights or a possum playing dead.

While many fears are rational, others are irrational and can hold us back from fully experiencing life. Rational fears involve imminent danger and pose an immediate physical threat to survival. These fears protect and help you avoid harm. For example, a fear of deep, choppy water will prevent you from swimming in turbulent waters to prevent drowning. Irrational fears, meanwhile, are genuine fears that pose little or no threat in reality; the danger is blown so out of proportion that it can take over your life. Let's take a look at a healthy fear of heights. Your fear of heights will come in handy to protect you from leaping like a daredevil down a giant flight of stairs. This fear turns into an irrational fear of heights when you won't even climb a flight of stairs or take an elevator. The belief is that something terrible will happen, so you avoid it.

Our limiting beliefs are fears we have about ourselves. They are often irrational because they aren't based in reality. Fear can also be an ally. It can convey to us what is holding us back. It can help open our awareness and show us where healing is needed. Let's take a look.

Inner Fears and Limiting Beliefs

If you believe you are smart, you are. If you think you are incapable, you are. If you believe the universe will support you, it does. If you think it's out to get you, you'll set up those types of scenarios. We become what we believe. Beliefs form our perceptions, which determine our choices and behaviors. Self-sabotaging beliefs are beliefs we have about ourselves that limit how we interact in the world. Our fears are connected to our belief system. We think that if we challenge or change the belief, we will be open and vulnerable to being harmed in some way. This is a false narrative we play over and over. Limiting beliefs are a result of living in the past. We make assumptions based on our past experiences and unresolved emotions.

Limiting beliefs are just that—restrictive and untrue. They are conditioned responses that control what we do in life. Many of our fears and limiting beliefs began in childhood, were not resolved, and follow us throughout our life. They limit our growth and happiness. These false beliefs are constantly directing our emotions and negative behaviors. Letting go of our limiting beliefs brings emotional freedom and allows us to be our true authentic self. When we do this, we move from fear to appreciating and loving who we are.

Letting go of our limiting beliefs brings emotional freedom and allows us to be our true authentic self.

Based on what we hear, see, and experience in childhood, we develop our core belief system about who we are in the world. By opening our awareness and observing our beliefs, we may just be able to pinpoint when particular limiting beliefs were formed. Our belief system becomes our inner critic, the inner voice that creates doubts and instills fear and feelings of inadequacy. Sometimes it's not clear which appeared first, the inner critic or the inner fear. Nonetheless, they are interrelated.

If you are not quite sure what your inner critic sounds like, try this experiment. Stand in front of a mirror naked and look at yourself. What comments do you hear coming from that inner voice in your head? Are they kind and loving words praising your essence and appearance? Or are you hearing an onslaught of criticisms about your imperfections with a list of instructions of what needs to be corrected? Most people hear some form of criticism.

When I did this, I knew I needed to shift my perceptions and make substantial changes in my beliefs. I was also afraid others would make fun of me. First, I accepted the changes that occurred in the body after an injury I incurred to both shoulders, which resulted in limited use of both arms and muscle loss. Next, I traced this belief back to childhood, hearing stories about what a scrawny, ugly baby I was from my grandfather. I didn't know it was a joke. I believed it to be true. I was surprised to discover that I had subconsciously carried this belief into adulthood. Once I knew I needed to be gentle and loving with myself, I acknowledged each area of the body that was subject to the wrath of my inner critic. I caressed or kissed (if I could reach it) each part and declared my new belief aloud, "I love you. You are a precious part of me." I no longer had the inner fear of being ridiculed. This was freedom.

It's helpful to delete those inner critic files that clutter the mind with false beliefs and harsh judgments and stir up our fears. Those files contain information that no longer serves you. Delete the files that put you down, create doubt, tell you that you are not special, or try to convince you that you will never make it in this world. Insert new files and change your pattern of thinking with thoughts that support loving yourself.

Here are some client examples of limiting beliefs and interrelated inner fears:

- "I won't ask for help because I can't trust others to complete the task." (Fear that other people can't be trusted.)

- "My marriage is suffering because my wife started working again and now she's never home." (Fear of being alone.)

- "I cannot do anything right because everything I touch gets ruined." (Fear that I will ruin something.)

- "I never wanted to go to the company party because I'm not much fun." (Fear that people won't like me.)

- "I'm fifty-six years old and struggle to be thin and need Botox treatments to compete in business because companies only hire young and attractive people." (Fear that I'm not good enough.)

Notice that a limiting belief often follows the word *because* with the reasons why. How often do we express a limiting belief and justify it with a *because*? I will share with you two limiting beliefs I let go:

"I do not let everyone know the real me because if they knew my whole story, they would judge me." Being real and exposing our vulnerabilities endears us with others. Others can identify with us. Birds of a feather flock together. When my belief shifted, I learned that my fears were unfounded.

Another one was, "I must strive for perfection because I am not good enough." For as long as I could remember, I would try to be impeccable and then demanding of myself to create great things. I was an overachiever with many accomplishments, beginning early on. My near-death experience twenty-five years ago changed how I saw life. Everything was already in perfect order. I just needed to release my ego's needs, trust in the Divine Source, and be aware of the opportunities before me. When I let go of perfection, I created even more with much less effort. (You'll have an opportunity to identify your own limiting beliefs in just a little while.)

Four Steps to Change Limiting Beliefs

To change a limiting belief, along with your thinking and behaviors around that belief, you need a new insight. Insights are born out of observing your thoughts. Detect the fear and the underlying feeling. When you realize you are afraid of something that is not there, you need to step outside the fear, detach from it, and observe it. Then you welcome a new insight, that aha moment that uncovers a new belief. You notice you no longer need to be affected by the old rooted belief with its fear-based attitudes and behaviors. Your new insight reveals that the old belief no longer serves your highest purpose, so you let it go. This helps build your resilience. Once you change your thinking, you need to stick with it and continuously remind yourself so that you do not fall back into your old belief.

I will guide you through a four-step process for changing a limiting belief using one of my clients as an example to illustrate the steps. Carol, a senior, lived alone in a condo that had multiple maintenance issues that needed to be fixed. After a month went by, I asked her why they hadn't taken care of the problems yet. She said she didn't ask them to come because she was afraid they would give her a hard time.

Step 1: Identify Your Limiting Belief

We talked and brought to light her fear and limiting belief that was holding her back. "I cannot ask for what I need because if I bother them, they will get angry and not like me." Carol was afraid to speak up. I asked her to observe her thoughts about this belief. When she observed her thoughts, she realized that her fear stemmed from her childhood. Her aunt, who had helped raise her, would often yell at Carol whenever she asked for something. Her aunt would say, "Go away. Can't you see that I'm busy." Her aunt would even add, "If you ask me again, I'm not going to love you anymore." I asked Carol what that meant. She replied, "It meant that I would not get what I need and/or be loved." I asked what would happen if she did not receive what she needed and she was not loved. Carol responded that she would be sad, hurt, and all alone.

Step 2: Question Your Belief

I asked Carol, "As a child, when your aunt told you to go away, even if she didn't really mean it, did it seem like she really wasn't going to meet your needs and that she wasn't going to love you anymore?" She said yes. It felt real. She was a little girl and, of course, she believed her aunt's words. Knowing how it felt to her as a child, I asked Carol if she could see her aunt not meeting her needs or not loving her anymore. She said she couldn't see that happening. When I asked her what she could see, she said she could see and hear her aunt saying the words. I asked Carol to speak her aunt's words out loud. As she was speaking them, Carol realized that her aunt's words weren't true. It was her belief in them that gave them meaning. Her aunt had always met her basic needs and did not stop loving her. Carol's belief no longer had the same meaning. For over fifty years, she thought that speaking up would cause her harm, her needs would not be met, and she would not be loved. Now, she knew that belief was false.

Step 3: Change Your Belief

Carol was ready to create a new belief. I asked if she had any insight into her experience. She replied, "Yes, I'm done with that old belief. I think I deserve a new one. I'm not too old to learn new tricks you know." I chuckled. She eagerly shared her new belief. She wanted to keep it short and easy to remember: "I am deserving and lovable." She later told me that she made a greeting card–size poster of it and put it on her refrigerator. I suggested she place one in her bathroom and on her nightstand, too. A few days later, she asked maintenance to fix the problems in her condo. They repaired everything within two days, and she was so happy. "They were as nice as they could be," she added.

Step 4: Strengthen Your New Belief

It was time for Carol to reinforce her new belief. I suggested she practice it and retrain her brain to accept her new thought. She had spent years forming the old belief, so it was only fair to give her new credence equal time so it would stick. I explained how to use her imagination and watch herself acting out this belief and new behaviors and habits. I told her to let it play like a movie in her mind. She told me she saw herself choosing the restaurant she wanted to go to instead of going where her friends picked, and they were okay with it. I encouraged her to continue practicing using different scenarios.

Like Carol, you can let go of your old limiting beliefs. However, sometimes it's hard to pinpoint those restricting beliefs. They can be hidden in the unconscious mind and may need some coaxing to show themselves. To help you uncover them, ask yourself a few questions. Where do you feel challenged? What do you want to change and what's stopping you? What are you struggling with and why? What do you perceive to be a problem? Notice what thoughts and situations arise as you ponder these inquiries. Be aware that when we live by our self-limiting beliefs, we also attract experiences to reinforce them and keep them alive.

When looking at our beliefs, we distinguish between what is valid and what is not true. For instance, believing that I am wet because I got caught in the rain is accurate. Believing that I am stupid because I didn't go to Harvard is not a true statement. Beliefs that are true usually don't change, whereas those that are false are changeable.

YOUR TURN FOR SELF-DISCOVERY

Self-limiting beliefs can hold you back. At one time in your life, these beliefs served a purpose. Now, some can be restrictive and provoke fear-based reactions. These negative emotions that monopolize the mind need to be questioned for their validity. It's your turn to dissolve the fear-producing thoughts that no longer serve you. Here are two exercises to begin your process in unraveling false beliefs. The second exercise may require more time and that's okay. It's not an easy task to change our limiting beliefs that have been a part of our life for a long time.

Self-Inquiry Exercise: Before you begin, find a quiet place and allow 10 minutes for this exercise. Close the eyes and take a few deep breaths to focus your awareness. When you feel relaxed and centered, gently open the eyes. In your journal, share three of your limiting beliefs by completing the following statement for each one: I cannot/won't/must (fill in the blank) because (fill in the blank), or just write down the problem: I am (fill in the blank) because (fill in the blank). As you use either or both approaches, do not judge or censor your thoughts and reasons.

Self-Inquiry Exercise: Before you begin, find a quiet place and allow 20 minutes for this exercise. Close the eyes and take a few deep breaths to focus your awareness. When you feel relaxed and centered, gently open the eyes and begin.

Choose one of the three limiting beliefs you identified and apply the four-step process in changing beliefs to create a new idea: 1) identify your limiting belief, 2) question your belief, 3) change your belief, and 4) strengthen your new belief. In your journal, process your belief and record your insights and comments. I encourage you to change your other limiting beliefs, too, when you are ready. In your journal, respond to the following prompts with your thoughts and insights:

- Where did the limiting belief come from and is it accurate and really true?

- What behaviors will you choose to reinforce your new belief?

- How will creating this new belief change your life? How will you benefit?

In Closing

Some fears and beliefs keep us safe and alive. Common sense tells us not to walk in front of a moving vehicle for fear we would be run over. There is not much that will convince us otherwise. We look for proof that supports our belief as true. Others may share the same belief, which further supports our opinion. Here are a few points to consider:

- When our fear becomes a false belief, it directs our emotions and negative behaviors and limits what we can do in life.

- We attract evidence that strengthens that limiting belief and ignore information that challenges that belief.

- Due to the fear of change, we will do whatever it takes to protect and keep false beliefs front and center. We can change this.

- Differentiate between well-founded beliefs and those that are not accurate.

Fear and limiting beliefs can be powerful catalysts for transformation. Through insight, you are able to transform fear-based false beliefs, knowing that they no longer serve your higher good. Positive beliefs about yourself and how you interact with the world help you to grow and feel happy. Deep down inside, you know you are greater than your limiting beliefs. As we grow and experience new challenges in life, don't be surprised if new self-limiting beliefs surface. It's a part of your evolution on your journey toward well-being. Trust in what your inner wisdom, your soul, is telling you.

In the next chapter, you will learn how to cultivate your relationship with yourself and others. You will discover your super strengths to build your resilience.

CHAPTER 15

The Art of Relationships

"Each friend represents a world in us, a world possibly not born until they arrive, and it is only by this meeting that a new world is born."
—ANAÏS NIN

Healthy and meaningful relationships begin with the relationship you have with yourself. Developing loving and trusting relationships starts with loving and trusting yourself. We teach others how to treat us. If we don't think our time is valuable, others won't either. If we talk negatively about ourselves, we give permission for others to do the same. If we don't speak up when we are being dealt with unfairly, we are letting others know that it's acceptable to walk all over us. Promoting a healthy relationship with ourselves is essential, so let's start there.

Relationship with Self

You are the most valuable relationship in your life. What does it take to be your own best friend? We must learn to say yes to our needs, encourage positive self-talk and self-love, set healthy boundaries, practice forgiveness, and develop our inner strengths.

Saying Yes to Me

How many times have you said you'll do something and then regret it later? Do you find yourself saying yes to other people when you really want to say no? We have all done this. It took a near-death experience and the lessons that followed for me to learn to comfortably say yes to me without a guilty conscious. It's in my nature to care and be there for others.

Did you grow up hearing no? "No, don't touch that," or "No running out into the street" or "No hitting your brother." The power of *no* formed our behaviors and conditioned responses and protected us from danger. As toddlers, we tested and learned how to use *no* to assert ourselves and build confidence. It was a healthy way to feel a sense of control. Along the way into adulthood, many of us lost our assertiveness and power to say no to others and situations. We put our own needs second.

When I found my voice again and spoke up for myself, I chose to say yes to me. I realized I could not blame anyone for my situation. How often do we play the victim role, blaming others for our misfortune? We are both the cause and the effect of what we experience. I needed to take responsibility for my decisions, actions, and choices. I realized that saying yes when I wanted to say no was a sign that I did not have healthy personal boundaries. Trying to please everyone resulted in weak boundaries. Part of my self-worth, at that time, came from people-pleasing and being needed. It was time to set stronger limits that coincided with my core values to protect myself from being used or controlled by the demands of others.

At first, saying no was uncomfortable. I was afraid of what others would think of me, so I gave excuses to explain myself. Using the word *because* after my *no* response was another way for me to defend my position. I was kidding myself. All I needed to do was say no without trying to defend, justify, or explain myself. Soon, it became easier and felt natural to honor me first.

I was assertive and direct in letting others know what behaviors toward me were acceptable and unacceptable. By saying no, I learned that placing other people's needs over my own needs was not a wise move. I switched my thinking and changed my behavior by listening to and acting on my heart's desires. Trusting in my intuition and connection with Divine Source guided me. It didn't eliminate my caring for others. I just needed to love and care for myself first so I could better care for others.

Promoting Positive Self-Talk

How often do you praise yourself? How often do you stress over all the things you've done poorly? Are you making snide remarks about yourself? The body listens to and responds to every word you say. Our words have power. Self-love and speaking kindly about yourself is vital to having a healthy relationship with yourself. Negative self-talk can encourage your inner critic. It can increase your stress levels and decrease your self-esteem. Negative self-talk usually starts in childhood and becomes a self-sabotaging habit. Be aware when your thoughts and the words you say are putting you down in any way. Would your best friend say those things to you? If not, then why would you? Notice when you are sounding like your own worst enemy and learn to be your own best friend.

To help you recognize your negative self-talk, listen to how you talk to yourself and how you talk about yourself to others. When you notice you are having a negative thought, follow these three action steps:

- Say "delete" to yourself silently or out loud.
- Choose to replace that thought with a positive one.
- Tell your inner critic to be quiet and go away. It has no place in your life anymore.

If you need help with this, you can ask a supportive friend or family member to point out when you are making derogatory remarks about yourself. Choose a code word like *blue* or *rose* that your friend can say to alert you when you are speaking negatively. When you hear your friend say your code word, be aware of what you said and follow the three action steps.

Looking on the brighter side of life helps promote positive self-talk while decreasing stress levels. Positive self-talk invites you to believe in yourself and see your strengths and abilities and all the good you have to offer. To move toward reducing negative self-talk, you can begin by opening your awareness to when and how often you are using belittling comments. Notice any correlations or triggers associated with these sabotaging one-liners. Then convert those remarks to more uplifting and encouraging ones. Phrases like "I can't do this" can shift to "How can I do this?" or "I'm no good at that" can switch to "How can I get better at that?" or "I'll never be able to go" can be replaced with "I'll check it out. Anything is possible."

Ask and Receive

Loving yourself is also asking for help and allowing others to help you. As I mentioned in Chapter 2, learning to delegate was imperative for my wellness. If you'd like, you can flip back to that chapter to review my suggestions. We are not in this world to try to figure it all out by ourselves. We were designed to be social and feel a sense of belonging. It's necessary for our survival to not be alone.

At the same time, knowing our limitations and when to ask for help is essential to prevent depleting our energy. Start with small, simple tasks until you feel more comfortable giving up control and then graduate to more challenging tasks. The more times you delegate, the easier it will be. Delegating tasks frees up your time and allows all involved to grow. It focuses on giving up control and letting go of perfection while trusting others to support a common goal.

Super Strengths

Building our inner resources strengthens our resilience. The more resilient we are, the better we are at coping with stress. Our inner resources, or as I like to call them, our Super Strengths, help us navigate and be adaptable through life. These Super Strengths are already inside you waiting to be discovered and developed. Everyone can cultivate inner resources. The more you use them, the stronger they become.

You may think you don't have any Super Strengths. That's just not true. You only need one to start. Have you ever gone to dinner, a movie, or anywhere by yourself or tried something new for the first time? That's courage. Were you ever given disturbing news and believed everything would turn out okay? That's faith. Have you ever been in an awkward situation and just started laughing? That's humor. Have you ever needed to solve a difficult problem? That can be intelligence or knowledge. Perhaps you felt in your gut that something was not right. That's intuition. Have you ever had a bright idea? That's creativity. Are you ready to rediscover your inner light?

Some of us know our strengths; others may be unsure. You may have just one inner resource you rely on. Here's a tip to help you discover and develop your Super Strengths. Hang out with positive, emotionally resilient people. Observe how they cope with life's challenges. Notice their inner resources and how they use them. If you are not able to recognize them, ask them and learn from them.

Self-Inquiry Exercise: Take a look at the list below of fifteen Super Strengths. In your journal, write down which ones you are already living as well as those you want to develop and add to your reservoir of resources. Feel free to come up with more than what is on this list.

Super Strengths

- Attitude
- Compassion
- Courage
- Curiosity
- Creativity
- Determination
- Faith
- Forgiveness
- Hope
- Honesty
- Humor
- Gratitude
- Integrity
- Intelligence
- Intuition
- Knowledge
- Optimism
- Passion

❖ Patience ❖ Self-Discipline ❖ Unconditional Love

Forgiveness

The topic of forgiveness can be a sensitive one. When we experience the feeling of anger from having been emotionally or physically hurt by another individual, we can be quick to blame and hold a grudge. Holding on to resentments for a long time can induce chronic stress and affect the cardiovascular and immune systems. When we cause hurt or harm to another, intentionally or accidentally, we can become defensive and attempt to turn the incident around to justify our behavior, as warranted.

Forgiveness is letting go of your ego's need to be right and take control. It's not about excusing the other's person's behavior or tolerating it in the future. Forgiveness creates inner strength by freeing yourself from the endless cycle of torment and hurt. The anger and pain you feel are your emotions and only affect you. You have the choice to hold on to them or let them go. Holding on to past anger only hurts and disempowers you. The past is the past. Staying in the memory of the past limits you and holds you back. Forgiveness is self-forgiveness and looks toward the future. Forgiveness is rooted in self-love.

Releasing the hurt through forgiveness starts by looking inward at yourself. Ask yourself, "What purpose does it serve me to hold on to the anger, hurt, or harm that has been caused? How is it affecting my health and well-being? How is it helping me move forward with ease and joy?" It's important to forgive yourself for any hurt or harm you may have caused the other person, intentionally or accidentally.

Then forgive and release the other person who co-created this incident with you. Also, be willing to ask for forgiveness. You are not giving in or condoning the situation. You are releasing them and setting yourself free from the debilitating bond you both share. As Nelson Mandela has said, "We forgive but not forgotten." You may never forget the incident. However, it will no longer dominate you.

Relationship with Others

Ideally, we surround ourselves with people who share a similar path and reflect our values. We attract like-spirited relationships. Healthy relationships are built on mutual trust and respect. When we embrace and accept our differences, we can dissolve the barriers that separate us and be open to conscious communication and discovery. Put yourself in someone else's shoes for a moment, even though you cannot possibly know what their story or life is truly all about, or what they may be actually feeling and thinking. Are you able to get a sense of what the other person is going through? Are you intently listening or just waiting to jump in and give your response? Sharing your love for another and having empathy help you appreciate others with greater understanding and awareness.

Not all relationships are healthy. Do you have unfinished emotional issues with people you find draining? The moment you remember that conflict, your thinking is in the past. The body believes the memory is real and responds physically and emotionally. Living in the past reinforces the inner conflict, robs you of your power, and prevents you from resolving and healing the problem. Unresolved emotional conflicts with another can fester and grow and cause suffering to everyone involved. So, it's helpful to learn to process your emotions as they are happening and free yourself from the pressures of holding on to the past. Conflict resolution begins with processing your feelings.

Pushing Buttons

When was the last time someone said something to you that triggered an emotional reaction? Many times it's someone close to you or a family member because they usually know what can set you off. When you feel someone is pushing your buttons, do you fight back and try to get even, keep your mouth shut, or stand your ground? The first thing to do when you realize your button has been triggered is to take responsibility for what you are feeling. It's your emotion; it's your button. The other person didn't cause your feeling. It was your choice to respond the way you did. It's an emotion that surfaced so it can be acknowledged, embraced, and accepted as part of you.

Next, notice when you have felt this feeling before. Are there any similarities? I suggest journaling your thoughts and insights. The same buttons tend to get pushed time and time again. Same button, different players. Ask yourself if your emotional response and interpretation of what happened serve your highest good. Do they allow you to grow or keep you stuck? This can be an opportunity to learn and heal and break the cycle of having the same buttons getting pushed again. During this process, remember to forgive yourself for being judgmental to you and the other person who co-created this scenario with you. If possible, share your experience with the person who participated in pushing your button. Let them know you are responsible for what you are feeling and not them. Share what you learned about yourself.

Processing your emotions in a healthy way and sharing your insights with the other person take bravery. It allows you to be real and express yourself without blame or feeling victimized. It's a gift that opens your relationships to a greater understanding. If the other person chooses to not resolve the situation and heal, you may find it necessary to be forgiving and part company amicably. When people no longer resonate with your highest good, it means that you have grown and can no longer relate. Living our highest good is what keeps us on our path moving toward our soul's purpose. At one point in your life, that relationship served you, and now it has changed for whatever reason. It doesn't mean that the other person is not a worthy person. You just no longer share much in common. Button pushers are some of our best teachers for our personal and spiritual growth.

Unconditional Love

Love is your divine essence that dwells within the lotus of the heart. Anger and fear separate us from love. Unconditional love is sharing your loving energy with another with no strings attached. It is not based on circumstance. There is no ego involvement or ulterior motive. When we try to control love, we place limits on its power to heal, unite, and experience joy. Understanding, tolerance, acceptance and mutual respect, and trust are some of the characteristics that unconditional love embraces. Expressing and experiencing love guides our thoughts, words, feelings, and deeds and gives life meaning and purpose.

YOUR TURN FOR SELF-DISCOVERY

Developing healthy relationships begins with you. Treating yourself with respect and appreciation is important. Trying to be like someone else or what someone else wants you to be is exhausting. It's easier to be yourself when self-love is your guiding light. As you learn more about yourself, you choose actions and behaviors to support your deepest desires and higher good. This crosses over into your relationships with others.

Self-Inquiry Exercise: Find a quiet place to sit and allow 10 minutes for this exercise. Close the eyes and take a few slow deep breaths through the nose to focus your awareness. Feel the air flowing through you. When you feel relaxed and centered, gently open the eyes. In your journal, respond to the following prompts with your thoughts and insights:

- As you recall your boundaries, what do you say yes to in your life?

- List at least one new personal boundary you choose to create that supports the life you desire.

- Reflect on your personal and professional life. Create a Super Me list by completing the statement "I am . . ." ten times with a positive quality about yourself. (For example, I am creative, I am honest, etc.) What are you proud of or what positive traits do you possess? If you cannot think of anything or if this feels uncomfortable, recall all of the kind comments and compliments you have received over the years.

- What gifts are unique to you? What makes you different from everyone else? It may be how you do something or the way you interact with others.

- Recall one person with whom you have unfinished business. Are you willing to close that loop of lingering disturbed energy? What plan are you committed to following to have closure?

- Name one or two people you believe have caused you harm and where forgiveness needs to happen.

- Name three people you don't often tell or show that you love them. Describe how and when you plan to tell them or show them.

In Closing

As you build healthy relationships, unconditional love is your true essence that you share with yourself and others. I encourage you to set your boundaries to protect yourself from the demands of others. Know that saying yes to yourself is a self-care practice that helps maintain mental, emotional, and physical wellness.

Conscious communication encourages you to speak and listen from the heart without judgment or blame. Clear any unfinished emotional business you have with others. If necessary, release relationships that no longer serve you. Develop your Super Strengths, your inner resources to help build your resilience and cope with life's challenges.

Congratulations on completing Part Four. You know how to

- Recognize which mismanaged anger styles you gravitate toward.

- Practice clearing emotional stress and dissolving anger.
- Begin letting go of self-destructive thoughts and associated fears.
- Develop and strengthen your inner resources to navigate through life.
- Cultivate a healthier relationship with yourself.
- Observe your relationships with others and notice where you can make improvements.

You are on the home stretch. Way to go!

PART FIVE

Elevate and Align Your Energy

"If you want to find the secrets of the universe, think in terms of energy, frequency, and vibration."
—NIKOLA TESLA

Scientists and modern technology have proven we live in an energetic world filled with frequencies and vibrations that affect us on every level. The words *energy, frequency,* and *vibration* are becoming household words in the twenty-first century. Understanding how to elevate yourself and align your energy with high-frequency living is vital. Our energetic vibration determines the quality of our mental, emotional, physical, and spiritual experiences with ourselves and others.

Have you ever felt drained after being around people who complain about one thing after another? When was the last time you were inspired and uplifted by another person? Would you like to have more sustainable energy so you can enjoy life more fully? We are constantly exchanging energy with others. Sometimes we give away our power and feel depleted or absorb other people's energy and feel either energized, calm, or drained.

As you approach your final steps toward your wellness transformation, Part Five will show you how you can work with the energy that surrounds you for healing and well-being. After completing the practices and self-inquiries, you will learn how to optimize your energy and balance the subtle energy system. Know how to create healing environments. Understand the importance of maintaining higher-vibration emotions. Explore how the sound and music can be used in your healing process.

CHAPTER 16

What's Energy Got to Do with It?

"If you are to thrive, you must participate in the evolution of your body's energy patterns."
—DONNA EDEN

We can sense and feel the surrounding energy. When you walk into a room full of people, can you feel the vibrations? Have you been able to tap into the vibes, the energy vibrations emitted by the people? Perhaps you feel more in tune with certain people over others. Energy is everywhere and affects all living beings. Energy and vibration levels can be high, low, or bounce between the two. In this chapter, you will discover your vibration level and how it relates to your overall well-being. You will learn to change, align, and balance your energy.

Human Energy Fields and Health

Each of us is an energy being made up of different vibratory frequencies. Our human energy field decides our state of health moment by moment as energy is continuously changing. It provides us with the blueprint for how we experience life, determining how we think, feel, act, and heal. In *A Practical Guide to Vibrational Medicine: Energy Healing and Spiritual Transformation*, Richard Gerber, MD, states,

"By realizing that human beings are energy, one can begin to comprehend new ways to view health and disease." All illness and healing begin in the energy fields.

The flow of energy creates either an in-balance or out-of-balance state. When the body is in balance, all systems are functioning optimally, and we can cope with life's stressors. When there is a disruption in the flow of energy, the organs and bodily systems are not able to defend against illnesses. We are not as equipped to handle stress, which impacts our physical health.

There are many causes of an imbalanced energy field that can disrupt our energy and state of well-being. Imbalances are reflected in the energy fields and can be detected before they show up as symptoms in the physical body. Disease means our energy is not flowing. Negative emotions can block the flow in the body. When you release and clear blocked energy, you open and restore the flow of energy, creating balance, harmony, and wholeness.

Low- and High-Energy Qualities

Our human energy fields vibrate at different frequencies and play a role in our health and the way we perceive our world. Each frequency has distinct mental, emotional, and physical qualities. Characteristics associated with lower vibrations are disempowering thoughts and behaviors, indecisiveness, pessimism, lack of concentration and purpose, and poor health and fatigue. Higher vibrations are associated with positive and empowering thoughts and behaviors, purposefulness, optimism, resilience, deep spiritual awareness, and a strong constitution.

Our energetic state affects our life and everyone around us. Each one of us has experienced both low and high energy. It's human nature to want to feel more high energy than low. However, for some, letting go of low-vibrational behaviors can be difficult. Yet, there is solace in knowing that we do have a choice over our thoughts, emotions, and behaviors. We choose the qualities that surround our soul's vibrational light. The more aligned our energy field is with higher vibrations, the more attuned we are with our higher Self. Being in the presence of a high-frequency vibration person is felt as "uplifting."

Low-Vibration Living

Low-vibration emotions can manifest into physical symptoms, create stress, and affect our energy. When our vibration is low, life seems harder. Even the simple things in life become problematic. People living with lower energy have a tendency to hold on to old hurts and resentments and can be overcritical and judgmental. They may feel like a victim and see life through tainted lenses. Continual moodiness, poor digestion, and feeling tired and sluggish (both mentally and physically) are common complaints. They lean toward seeing their world as a glass half empty by putting a negative spin on a situation rather than a glass half full and seeing the brighter, positive side. Living with negativity stops the movement of energy. Our energy needs to flow and function at its optimal best to feel a sense of well-being.

Important Note: Some low-energy traits like depression may require professional assistance to resolve. If you are depressed or need added support, seek the advice of a mental health professional.

Rachel's Story

Rachel was feeling like her "life was going nowhere" and "everything was a strain." She did not like her high-pressure, high-paying job, and stayed because she did not have the energy to look for something else. When I asked her to name one thing she liked about her job, she quickly replied, "Nothing, it's all out the window."

Going for a drink with friends after work "filled up her time." She spent most of that time complaining about her life. One by one, her friends distanced themselves after she consistently made critical and jealous comments about how they were living their lives. She was belligerent to coworkers and said her situation was a result of the problems she was having with this person or that person because they didn't appreciate her.

When her constant low-vibration behavior transferred over to her family, they gave her an ultimatum. They told her to change the way she was acting, or she would not be welcome at family gatherings. This ultimatum led Rachel to work with me. She was ready to make a change.

Rachel knew she was pushing away the people who cared about her. When she realized her behavior stemmed from her unhappiness, she began to look inward at her feelings and desires. Her eye-opening, aha moment was when she realized it wasn't the particular job she disliked. It was her career choice. She was following family tradition and doing what she thought she was supposed to do. The moment her awareness opened to allow her to do whatever made her happy without feeling like she was betraying her family, she felt relieved. She let go of the underlying anger she had toward her parents and siblings. Much to her surprise, her family supported her in her dream for a different life. Rachel then saw her high-paying job as a blessing. Her plan now was to negotiate fewer hours with less pay so she could spend more time pursuing her interests. Once she found her calling, she would transition and step into her new business.

High-Vibration Living

Living a high-frequency vibration life is filled with light, unconditional love and joy, and aligned with Divine Source. Self-aware, self-disciplined, vibrant, creative, playful, and intuitive with a sense of purpose are high-vibration living qualities. People with higher energy appear to have everything working in their favor, like being in the right place at the right time and being a team player. They draw opportunities that support their desires and goals in life. They feel a sense of happiness and thrive even during difficult times because they look for solutions. Higher-energy people attract and match the energies of other high-vibration people. They are less likely to be adversely affected by lower negative vibrations and stressful situations.

Grace's Story

Grace, a client, managed to shift her low vibration to high. Her life was hectic, juggling family and job responsibilities while maintaining an active social life. It appeared to others that she had it all. Inside, she felt her life was going nowhere and she was a victim of circumstance. Changes in her daily routine were met with hidden bouts of impatience and irritability. She kept her feelings to herself so others would not know the negativity that was brewing and taking over many of her thoughts. She requested my services because she wanted to live a purposeful and meaningful life.

Together, we began working on her becoming more self-aware and self-reflective. Over time, her behaviors became a lifestyle change that she was committed to keeping. She has a better handle on her thoughts, emotions, and feelings and is rarely overwhelmed by life's trials and tribulations. Life flows more naturally for her as she trusts her decisions. She is focused and clear about what she wants in life and can express her creativity through her many talents. People find her to be an inspiration and want to hang out with her. She cares about others in her life. Words like *grateful*, *trustworthy*, and *giving* describe her personality. She recognizes the importance of having joy in life and jokes about life's little ups and downs. Grace says she now lives, as she calls it, a soul-centered life.

Be Aware of Your Vibration

Are you living a low- or high-vibration life? You may have traits of both. Our energy is continually changing. Observe yourself and notice which characteristics you possess from the descriptions offered earlier. Be aware of your thoughts, feelings, and behaviors, and when your vibration is low, make a conscious effort to change it. Everyone has the potential to align his or her spiritual vibration to resonate with the light of Spirit. Everything you are reading and practicing in this book is about living a high-vibration life to help you reach your fullest potential.

It's easy to get pulled down by chronic stress or low-energy situations and people. Fortunately, there are behaviors and practices you can do to balance your energy and align or realign with a higher vibration. It's essential that we tune in and take control of the energies in and around us. Otherwise, our environment can control our lives if we allow it. The following three practices, which I teach my clients and personally use daily, can help you strengthen and protect your energy.

Practice: Tapping into Your Energy

The energy technique I use a couple of times a day to strengthen my immune system and restore my energy involves tapping or thumping the thymus gland. The thymus gland is the body's master gland located a little above the center of the sternum (breast bone) between the lungs and in front of the heart. Using either your bunched-up fingers or knuckles, vigorously thump this area of the sternum for 20 seconds to stimulate the thymus gland. Breathe in through the nose and out through the mouth as you are tapping.

Practice: Earthing and Grounding Your Energy

When was the last time you were barefoot or had your toes in the grass? Connecting with nature is essential for our well-being. A practice called earthing (or grounding) encourages walking barefoot to reconnect with the earth's electrical energy. The feet absorb electrons that help neutralize the free radicals known to cause inflammation in the body. Grounding has been shown to improve sleep, decrease pain and inflammation, lessen fatigue, and reduce stress and anxiety. This natural lifestyle practice may be just what the doctor, or in my case, what the nurse ordered.

Unfortunately, many have sacrificed the great outdoors for indoor and high-rise living, disconnecting us from our roots, literally. Are you one of the many who have switched from wearing natural leather-soled shoes to a more flexible plastic or rubber-soled shoes like sneakers? Synthetic materials are insulators that act as a barrier to earth's electrons being absorbed by the body through the feet.

Some surfaces are suitable for earthing, while others block the energy. You can ground yourself on grass, dirt, beach sand, and unsealed concrete but not asphalt. Indoors you can be earthing on unglazed ceramic tile or unpainted and unsealed concrete but not on carpet, wood, laminate, or vinyl surfaces. These surfaces are not conductive, meaning the earth's electrical charge cannot pass through.

Consider setting aside time to walk barefoot as part of your daily ritual. As you are earthing, take a moment and stand in stillness. Feel the feet sinking into the earth, grounding you. Imagine breathing up through the soles of the feet, drawing the energy up to the heart and filling the heart center with the love of nature.

Practice: UpFlow Technique

Most of us have encountered a situation with someone voicing a complaint by raising their voice in anger. What do you do? Matching that energy and participating in a heated exchange are not constructive and will only escalate the negativity in a powerplay. I created a practice called the UpFlow Technique. It teaches you how to keep your vibration level up and your energy flowing to stay balanced in these circumstances. Instead of being reactionary, you remain focused and calm so that you can respond accordingly. Here are the three steps for this technique:

* Reserve your energy and keep the body relaxed by dropping the shoulders and relaxing the jaw. As you are listening to the person making their point, have direct eye contact and be aware of your breath. Observe and follow the out breath to the end. Wait for the momentary pause before you breathe in again. When we get upset, we tend to shorten the breath, breathe more shallowly or rapidly, or even hold the breath. You can now be fully present, centered, and calm.

* As you continue to relax and breathe, acknowledge the other person. Let them know you are consciously listening to every word they are saying. Use body language like nodding your head occasionally or using facial gestures. Be sure to keep your body posture open and not cross your arms over your chest. You can make comments like "mm-hmm" without interrupting them. Let them have center stage until they are empty with nothing more to say. In doing this, you do not compete with the other person's energy or become reactive or defensive. You let the negative energy flow past you and focus on the positive energy within you.

* After the person has finished expressing themselves, you can enter the conversation with your higher vibration. Most times, you will notice the other person's energy settle down, having been in the

presence of your calm and relaxed demeanor. An energetic shift has most likely occurred. Now a constructive conversation may be possible.

Practice the UpFlow Technique during regular, non-heated conversations. In this way, when unprovoked anger or complaints come your way, you can be better prepared to apply steps one and two in a matter of seconds.

Energy Drainers

We've all been there on one side or the other. You engage in conversation with someone only to find that the discussion is sad and depressing. All you want to do is to escape, but for whatever reason, you cannot. You end up feeling completely drained after your interaction. This person may be suffering and spiraling downward. They may be unintentionally trying to manipulate you for personal gain. Either way, their energy can adversely affect you. How do you know which people will deplete your energy? First, you need to know what to notice.

Energy drainers hold all positions in society. Perhaps it's a business colleague, family member, close friend, or a person you meet in line at the grocery store pouring their heart out. These people may not be aware of how they are stuck in their perpetual story filled with hardships. Some may not be ready or know how to let go of their suffering. Their story may be a way they define themselves, and without it, they would feel lost. As we listen to them, it's helpful to know we are only hearing a part of the equation and do not have all the facts. Knowing this, we can be supportive without feeling trapped and pulled in and becoming part of the other person's story.

Another type of energy drainer needs other people's energy to survive. Insecure in themselves, they tend to monopolize the conversation to build themselves up. They are usually oblivious of their controlling behavior. They like to hypnotize others with praise and then entice others to do whatever they need regardless of how it might adversely affect the others. These energy drainers often have magnetic personalities, are proud, appear overconfident, and usually hold positions of power.

Energy drainers can also be extremely peppy, bouncing-off-the-walls-type people. Their enthusiasm is over the top. You may be sensitive to it. Being in their presence or in the company of overly excited groups of individuals can be exhausting. Have you ever gone to a concert or sporting event with screaming fans only to leave feeling beaten up and worn out when you arrived home? You may have absorbed the overpowering energy of the group. Some individuals even find being in a crowd of people tiring, even if it's a positive interaction.

Protect Your Energy

You know you were in the presence of an energy drainer if you felt vibrant, confident, and happy before your interaction and then felt sad, irritable, embarrassed, or emotionally depleted when you parted company. However, people can only drain your energy if you let them. So how do you remove their hold on you and interact with these individuals in a healthy manner? Keep your energy vibration high, set your boundaries, and refuse to be pulled into their drama by playing the victim role. In some situations, you may need to be straightforward and express your feelings and listen to their response. You can show support by being kind, loving, and compassionate during your interaction.

Anchoring Energy with NLP

What if you could choose to feel calm and relaxed under most any circumstance whenever you wish? This feeling is possible using a neuro-linguistic programming (NLP) technique known as anchoring. NLP teaches approaches to increase self-awareness and communication and to improve mood, emotion, state of mind, and brain behavior.

Anchors represent stability and security. We can intentionally set up emotional anchors. In NLP, anchoring creates an association between a particular emotion or behavior with a specific touch or trigger so that feeling can be accessed at a later time.

You may have formed anchors in your life naturally. One example would be when you hear a piece of music, and you immediately feel happy for no particular reason. At some point, you set up a link between that specific piece of music and a feeling of happiness. Maybe the smell of freshly baked cookies makes your mouth water with a sense of warmth and love.

When you are experiencing low energy or stress emotions, you can trigger and replace these feelings with positive emotions and responses. You can set an anchor for any emotion or state of mind. The following self-inquiry exercise will lead you through a process to set up an anchor for relaxation.

Self-Inquiry Exercise: Before you begin, choose an anchoring touch. Perhaps hold a finger with the opposite hand or place a hand on the chest over the heart. Choose a touch you feel is comfortable for you. Now find a quiet place and allow 5 minutes for this exercise. Close the eyes and take a few deep breaths to focus your awareness.

Now imagine or recall a moment in your life when you felt completely calm and relaxed with no distractions. When a memory comes to mind, go inward, and feel yourself being there as if you are reliving it. Use all of your senses to make it as real as possible. Listen to what you hear. Notice what you see. Be aware of any aromas. How do you physically and emotionally feel?

When you feel completely engaged inside this memory, activate and secure the feeling in the body by using your anchoring touch. Place your hand over your heart or hold your finger. After a few seconds or as soon as that feeling begins to dissipate, release the anchoring touch and open the eyes. If you were able to relive the memory fully, you set the anchor.

After 10 to 15 seconds, you can test it by applying the anchor and noticing if you can retrieve that calm and relaxed state of mind again.

You may need to repeat this procedure a few times to achieve the desired response. Later on, you can summon this feeling in a controlled way whenever you want by using your anchor touch.

Note: Your anchoring touch may not work with certain emotional situations, such as extreme fear or severe clinical depression. Other additional approaches may be needed first to lessen the degree of anxiety or intense sadness before using the anchoring technique.

YOUR TURN FOR SELF-DISCOVERY

A high-vibration life is filled with unconditional love and joy and is aligned with Divine Source. The higher your vibration, the more powerful your ability to attract positive energy and the less likely you are to be affected by stressful situations. It's your turn to take a closer look at what can influence your energy.

Self-Inquiry Exercise: Before you begin, find a quiet place and allow 10 minutes for this exercise. Close the eyes and take a few deep breaths to focus your awareness. When you feel relaxed and centered, gently open the eyes. In your journal, respond to the following prompts with your thoughts and insights:

- Are you attracting positive, vibrant people or surrounding yourself with energy-draining individuals? Make a list of the primarily high-vibration people and habitually low-vibration people in your life and notice which list has more names.

- Write about your experiences using the three energy alignment practices you learned in this chapter: Tapping into Your Energy, Earthing, and UpFlow Technique.

- List the energy drainers in your life. Choose one action step to protect your energy and write it down.

- Were you able to relive a calm and relaxing memory and set up your anchor? Were you able to retrieve the calm and relaxed state of mind? What was your experience?

In Closing

So, what's energy got to do with it? Everything. As you learned, living a higher-vibration life has its benefits. It invites like-spirited people and higher-vibration opportunities into your life. Positivity, optimism, and creativity are reflected in your thoughts, choices, and behaviors. Love and life flow more easily. Purpose guides your desires to succeed. You choose to live more joyfully in alignment with the light of your higher Self and Divine Source. Here are some key points to remember:

- It's essential to be aware of your energy and know whether you are vibrating at a low or high frequency.

- Recognize the energetic qualities of the people you associate with and decide who you want in your life. Align your energy and surround yourself with high-vibration family, friends, and associates who elevate you and challenge you to grow and be your best.

- Boost your energy and immune system by tapping the thymus gland.

- Connect with the energy of the earth and nature and have fun in the process.

- Recognize when to use the UpFlow Technique to shift your shared energy with a negative individual. Create a higher vibration to stay balanced and calm so as not to absorb the other person's energy.

- Know when you are encountering an energy drainer and take steps to protect your energy.

✣ Use the anchoring technique to access relaxation at will.

This chapter served as an introduction to understanding how energy determines how we experience life. There is much more to be said. In the chapters to follow, you will learn more approaches to balance and living harmoniously, starting with a look at the body's energy centers.

CHAPTER 17

Healing Through the Chakras

"To achieve excellence, we must also consider and work with what is not apparent, with what cannot be seen. We must journey into the complex world of subtle energies."

—CYNDI DALE

We are spiritual and energetic beings. We may not be able to see energy fields with the naked eye, but we know they are there. The human energy field can have a profound impact on wellness. Disruptions in the flow of energy can result in illness. While assessing our subtle energy anatomy, we can observe potential problems early on and introduce and combine holistic approaches along with modern medicine to restore health.

The human energy field is made up of physical, mental, emotional, and spiritual bodies, or layers. Our main human energetic system is known as the chakra system. Ancient teachings describe these spiritual energy centers as vortices, or wheels of light, that are located along the spinal column and act as transformers and antennae shifting energy from low vibration to high and vice versa. They collect and convert the streams of magnetic energies from the earth and universal energies that sustain life and that can be used by the human body for the functioning of the body. The chakras connect with the physical and energetic bodies through the nervous and endocrine (hormonal) systems.

Physical and mental stress and illness can close the chakras and flow of energy. It's vital to keep our energy centers open, activated, and balanced. Now let's take an introductory look at each of the chakras.

Chakras

The ancient yogic traditions of India considered the healing energy and state of balance of the chakra system to be an indicator of health and a path to wellness. There are seven major and many minor chakra centers in the body, and they play an active role in every part of your life. This is a quite broad topic, so I will explore with you just the major chakras that manage our most vital functions and essential needs, and how we can use them in healing.

I first started learning about the chakras in 1979 when I was studying Jain meditation with Gurudev Shree Chitrabhanu. Together with his teachings, his book *The Psychology of Enlightenment: Meditation on the Seven Energy Centers* was my guide. I found the path to help my healing process and spiritual development was deeply rooted in understanding and working with the chakras, the physical, emotional, and spiritual bodies, and connecting with Divine Source.

The seven major chakras are located along the central axis of the body from the base of the spine to the top of the head. These energy centers are more like an area of the body where consciousness and matter meet rather than an exact pinpoint on the body. Chakras are integrated energy centers that influence our mental, emotional, physical, and spiritual well-being. The chakras are not physical. They are a part of consciousness that works together with our biofield and physical body through the endocrine and nervous systems.

Each chakra reflects certain qualities of our personality and regulates the functions of those body organs associated with that chakra. They have their own energetic frequencies. The chakras located lower in the body vibrate slower, and those higher up in the body vibrate faster. These frequencies also correlate with visible color light ranging from red with the lowest vibration to violet with the highest vibration.

Our life's experiences and stories, as well as our emotional, physical, and spiritual memories, are collected and stored in our chakras. As Donna Eden, in her book *Energy Medicine,* reveals, "Memory is energetically coded in your chakras just as it is chemically coded in your neurons. An imprint of every emotionally significant event you have experienced is recorded in your chakra energy." Both positive and negative stressful beliefs about past events are held in storage until we are ready to deal with them. Each chakra holds a part of your story. The chakras need to be clear and energetically connected to function adequately. Releasing energetic blocks allows the chakras to resonate and your life to flow. As the story unfolds, a new chapter can emerge.

The chakras need to be clear and energetically connected to function adequately.

In the following sections, I'll provide some basic details about each of the chakras so that you can begin to familiarize yourself with these qualities and perhaps identify where you may be blocked. This information will be helpful as you take steps to restore balance. It's important to note that there is no set way to activate and open the chakras. Trust your intuition and choose the approaches that feel appropriate for you.

Root Chakra

The root chakra is located at the base of the spine between the genitals and the anus, known as the perineum. It is associated with our survival instincts and our fight/flight/freeze response. It helps structure our foundation and controls our physical existence. We feel secure when our basic needs of food, shelter, clothing, and financial security are met. It's also related to our sexual functions.

When the first chakra is in balance, we feel safe, secure, connected, and grounded. We can manage our lives with ease. When it is blocked and out of balance, we may have low energy with a lack of vitality. Perhaps we feel trapped in our job or career, or afraid that our income will not be enough to cover inflating costs. We can become fearful and anxious that our needs will not be met.

The adrenals are linked with this chakra. Some physical signs that there is a block are constipation, hemorrhoids, degenerative arthritis, and leg pain. It is associated with the sense of smell, corresponding element earth, and the mantra sound *Lam*. The color of the root chakra is red.

Energy-Balancing Tips for the Root Chakra

- Self-care: Refer to Chapters 9 and 10.
- Be in nature and ground yourself. Go barefoot in the grass.
- Use aromatherapy from flowers, herbs, bushes, and trees to connect with nature.
- Play the drum or listen to drumming music.
- Wear red clothing or red toenail polish.
- Eat red foods (e.g. apples, strawberries, and grapes).
- Eat root vegetables (e.g. sweet potatoes, onions, carrots, and beets).
- Gift yourself red flowers.

Sacral Chakra

The sacral chakra is located a few inches below the navel. This is our emotional center where our creativity is cultivated, and new projects are born. It's about how we express our feelings and creativity in the world. Our need for love is nurtured, and our sexual and sensual energies and desires explored.

When the second chakra is open and balanced, we feel a sense of vitality and happiness. We guide our life force toward meeting our needs and goals. We're comfortable with ourselves and our relationships.

When it is blocked, we flounder in search of creative solutions. Feelings of guilt and emotional insecurity may surface. Opening up in relationships can be hard.

The ovaries and testes are linked with this chakra. Some physical signs that there is a block are low back pain, reproductive concerns, sexual issues, and urinary tract infections. It is associated with the sense of taste, corresponding element water, and the mantra sound *Vam*. The color of the second chakra is orange.

Energy-Balancing Tips for the Sacral Chakra

- Swim or relax in a bath.
- Listen to the ocean or water fountains.
- Play, splash, and laugh in the water and have a water fight.
- Help stay emotionally calm with yoga, tai chi, or qigong.
- Wear orange clothing.
- Eat orange foods (e.g., sweet potatoes, cantaloupe, pumpkin, and carrots).
- Gift yourself orange flowers.

Solar Plexus Chakra

The third center, the solar plexus chakra, is located below the sternum. It's our personal power center and is about intellect, control, and identity. This center is concerned with feeling and thinking, and about setting goals to achieve our desires and ambitions.

When in balance, we trust our "gut" feelings to help guide our decisions. We radiate confidence in who we are and in what we can offer so we can achieve our life purpose. When the energy is blocked, uncertainty and indecision take over. We feel like victims. We feel powerless and lack a healthy sense of self-esteem.

The pancreas is the endocrine gland linked with this chakra. Some physical signs that there is a block are digestive, intestinal, and organ disorders. It is associated with the sense of sight, corresponding element fire, and the mantra sound *Ram*. The color of the third chakra is yellow.

Energy-Balancing Tips for the Solar Plexus Chakra

- Be in sunshine 20 minutes a day, but avoid the high-intensity sun between 10 a.m. and 4 p.m.
- Light candles.
- Use color and lighting to enhance the mood in your home and work space.
- Listen to music featuring the oboe or clarinet.
- Wear yellow clothing.
- Eat yellow foods (e.g., lemons, bananas, grapefruit, summer squash, and spaghetti squash).
- Gift yourself yellow flowers.

Heart Chakra

The heart center is located in the middle of the chest and is about love, compassion, forgiveness, and healing. Understanding, tolerance, and acceptance live here. The heart chakra corresponds with close heartfelt relationships.

When in balance, we feel a sense of harmony and peace with ourselves and others. The heart chakra balances the three lower male energy centers with the three upper female energy centers. Being androgynous, the heart is balanced with both feminine and masculine energies. Our heartbeat aligns with the rhythm of the universe. When out of balance, the heart hardens and closes off to love. We can be needy and clingy in relationships or hold grudges.

The thymus gland and cardiac and respiratory systems are linked with this chakra. Some physical signs that there is a block are asthma, lung and heart conditions, and upper back pain. It is associated with the sense of touch, the corresponding element air, and the mantra sound *Yam*. The color of the heart chakra is green, and the higher heart chakra is pink.

Energy-Balancing Tips for the Heart Chakra

- Relax and breathe.
- Reach out to others with kindness.
- Receive a massage and affectionate touch.
- Listen to music featuring strings like the violin or harp.
- Wear green or pink clothing.
- Eat green foods (e.g., limes, kiwi, broccoli, celery, avocado, leafy greens, and green beans).
- Gift yourself pink flowers or a green plant.

Throat Chakra

The throat chakra is the center for self-expression; it opens us to more profound wisdom and our soul. It's about speaking our truth, asserting our voice, and sharing our creativity with the world. Expressing our creativity can be sharing our artistic talents in music, dance, art, or writing. It can be manifesting what we think, feel, or desire in life with discernment.

When in balance, we feel comfortable knowing what to say and when and assured that our voice is heard with clarity and strength. We can express ourselves with fluidity and ease. When this center is blocked, our communication and creativity suffer. We are lost for words and afraid to speak our mind.

The thyroid and parathyroid are the endocrine glands linked with this chakra. Some physical signs that there is a block are chronic sore throat, temporomandibular joint pain (TMJ), thyroid issues, tinnitus, and neck pain. The color of the throat chakra is blue. This center is associated with the sense of hearing, corresponding element ether (space), and the mantra sound *Ham*. There are no further references to the physical senses or elements after this chakra. The higher chakras are dedicated to our spiritual essence and our Divine existence.

Energy-Balancing Tips for the Throat Chakra

- Sing, hum, or chant.
- Listen to the sounds of nature like birds, wind, or insects.
- Laugh and tell jokes.
- Listen to flute music.
- Wear blue clothing.
- Eat blue foods (e.g., blueberries, blue corn, and Adirondack blue potatoes).
- Gift yourself blue flowers.

Third Eye or Brow Chakra

The sixth chakra is located in the center of the forehead between and slightly above the eyebrows. It is the center for intuition, deeper self-knowledge, and self-realization. Tapping into our inner sight allows us access to our deeper spiritual truth, insights, and inner light. We can tune in to the energy around us.

When in balance, we are aware of our purpose and the motivations underlying our actions. We connect with a deeper meaning behind the events of our life. When this chakra is blocked, we may doubt ourselves, close off from our truth, become indecisive, and make poor decisions. We lack clarity and can feel lost with no sense of purpose.

The pituitary is the endocrine gland linked with this chakra. Some physical signs that there is a block are headaches, sinusitis, blurred vision, and eyestrain. It is associated with the inner sound *Sham,* and the color indigo.

Energy-Balancing Tips for the Brow Chakra

- Draw or paint and use your imagination.
- Practice meditation and visualization.
- Listen to chimes, singing bowls, or Tibetan bowls.
- Wear indigo, dark blue, or deep purple clothing.
- Eat blueish purple foods (e.g., blackberries, figs, acai, dark plums, and eggplant).
- Gift yourself purple flowers.

Crown Chakra

Located at the top of the head, the crown chakra is the center for higher knowledge, higher purpose, and our divinity. It is the link between our material and spiritual realms. This center is like a receiver. Energy, information, and wisdom are drawn inward through the crown, which is then disseminated throughout the chakras and the body.

When this center is open, we are free to receive inspiration. We are aware of being connected with something bigger than ourselves. Our experience of unity with the Divine Source lends itself to feeling at peace and at one with all of creation. When this chakra is blocked, we may feel alone and isolated, and disconnected from spirit. We may find ourselves identifying more with the ego self and feeling attached to possessions, positions, people, and money.

The pineal is the endocrine gland linked with this chakra. Some physical signs that there is a block are insomnia, neurological disorders, and sensitivity to light and sound. The mantra for the seventh chakra is the universal sound, the inner sound *Aum,* pronounced *Om.* The colors associated with this chakra are violet, white, or gold.

Energy-Balancing Tips for the Crown Chakra

- Pray and meditate.
- Be mindful and grateful.
- Wear white, violet, or gold clothing.
- Eat violet or white foods (violet: e.g., plums, purple asparagus, and red cabbage; white: e.g., white onions, cauliflower, white mushrooms, and yogurt).
- Gift yourself violet or white flowers.

Chakra Affirmations

We can use affirmations to enliven the chakras. With your attention on a particular chakra, repeat each phrase with the intention that the chakra is being energetically activated with these words of encouragement. You can use the following expressions or create your own.

Chakra	Affirmation
Root	I am protected, secure, and grounded.
Sacral	I am centered, creative, and passionate.
Solar Plexus	I am successful, courageous, and loved.
Heart	I am open to love, compassion, and joy.
Throat	I express my purpose creatively and clearly.
Third-Eye	I am intuitive and connected with my inner wisdom.
Crown	I am at peace and one with all of life.

YOUR TURN FOR SELF-DISCOVERY

Balancing the chakras encourages you to get in touch with the body to look at the symptoms and causes of a concern or problem and discover which chakra is not functioning adequately. You can then apply the appropriate healing energy and approaches for that particular chakra.

Self-Inquiry Exercise: Close the eyes and take a few deep breaths to focus your awareness. Bring your attention to each chakra. Notice how each chakra feels and bring to your awareness any concerns you have related to that chakra. Then open the eyes, and begin. In your journal, respond to the following prompts with your thoughts and insights:

- Are you aware of any of your chakra(s) that are blocked or leaking energy? Which ones?
- What symptoms and imbalances are you feeling?
- What rebalancing approaches did you or will you use?
- What shift in energy, thought, or feeling did you experience after trying the rebalancing approach?
- Practice the following chakra meditation. It is a guided imagery meditation for healing and activating your energy flow. The effect of imagery on healing is well documented. The use of visualization with color or light enhances the healing process. The use of sound in healing is also very powerful. Each center has a specific sound vibration, or mantra. You will be using these healing color and sound vibrations to consciously activate and raise your energy level in these centers. Verbally toning these sounds enlivens the chakras. As you use the breath, and sound the mantra aloud, you infuse the breath of life into the healing process. Have the intention to consciously open these centers to allow energy to flow freely. After completing the meditation, record your experience and insights.

Chakra Meditation

Before you begin, find a quiet place and allow 35 minutes for this exercise. Listen to the 30-minute chakra meditation. Afterward, spend 5 minutes to slowly come back to present-moment awareness. Then resume your activities or, if you prefer, rest. You may record this meditation for personal use and play it back to follow along. Speak slowly and let your voice soothe you. If you record it on your smartphone, silence the ringer and any alerts when you play it back.

Place yourself in a comfortable position with the head and neck and spine straight. Make certain the body is well supported. Gently close the eyes. Breathe in and out through the nose. Let go of any tension. Release the jaw, letting the lips and teeth part slightly. Allow the breath to flow naturally and easily. Invite the body to relax and let go, as you remain awake and alert.

Now direct your attention to the base of the spine. This is the first energy center. It is the root center or root chakra. It's related to the physical world, to our basic survival instincts. When you connect to this grounding energy, you feel connected to all of life and have faith that your basic needs will be met.

Now imagine a fuzzy red ball of light at the base of the spine. Picture this ball of light. Feel it begin to pulsate, alive with energy. With this energy, have the intention of opening this center. The sound vibration for this chakra is LAM. Now take a deep breath, and as you exhale, let this healing vibration be released from the base of the spine into the environment. Sound this mantra aloud one to three times.

Allow your attention to move upward to the genital area, the second chakra. This center is related to sexuality, all relationships, creativity, and work. When we enliven this area, we begin to observe each person in our life as having a spiritual purpose. We connect with all our creative energies so we can create meaningful partnerships and fulfilling work in our lives.

Now imagine an orange ball of light in this area. As you visualize this ball of light, watch it slowly begin to revolve. As it gently spins, it grows larger. Fill this center with the healing energy in this light. The sound vibration for the second chakra is VAM. Take a deep breath, and as you exhale, let this sound flow out from this area into the surroundings. Sound this mantra aloud one to three times.

Gradually move your awareness farther up to the solar plexus area. The third chakra is associated with our power, the ego, our self-esteem. Activating this energy center releases our power to fulfill our desires and our passions and achieve our goals with integrity.

Now imagine a sphere of yellow light around this area. Brilliant yellow light. Feel the warmth, the energizing power. As you breathe into this center, the light becomes brighter and brighter. Brilliant yellow light. The sound vibration for the third chakra is RAM. Take a deep breath, and as you exhale, let this sound flow out from this area into the environment. Sound this mantra aloud one to three times.

Gently place your attention in the middle of the chest, the heart chakra, or fourth energy center. It is related to love, compassion, and our healing energy. When this energy flows freely, we connect to the power of love. We extend heartfelt compassion, forgiveness, and love toward others in our life and also ourselves.

Now imagine a beautiful green light illuminating the heart center. Visualize its radiance. Breathe into this light. Beautiful green light. Absorb its essence, its healing energies. As you breathe out, let this light expand in all directions. The sound vibration for the fourth center is YAM. As you exhale, have the intention for this sound to emerge from the heart chakra into the world. Sound this mantra aloud one to three times.

Slowly move your attention to the area of the throat. This fifth chakra is connected with our self-expression and purpose in life. We can feel when we have a block in this center. We refer to it as a "lump in the throat." Activating this center allows us to clearly express ourselves, releasing our power in the world.

Now visualize the throat bathed in sky blue light. Feel the soothing light. As you breathe into this center, the light becomes brighter and brighter. Feel the soothing light opening this area, creating more space for energy to flow effortlessly. The vibration for the fifth chakra is HAM. As you exhale, allow the sound to resonate from the throat chakra into the environment. Sound this mantra aloud one to three times.

Bring your awareness to the area of the forehead between the eyebrows. The sixth center, known as the third eye or mind chakra, is related to insight, intuition, and wisdom. When we consciously activate this center through attention and intention, we discover the deeper truth around the events in our lives.

Now imagine the third eye chakra immersed in an indigo ball of light. A radiant bluish-purple light. As you visualize this ball of light, feel it pulsate, alive with energy. Allow it to expand. The sound vibration, the mantra for the sixth chakra, is SHAM. As you exhale, let the sound emanate from this insight chakra into the surroundings.

Allow your awareness to move to this seventh chakra located at the crown or the top of the head. This center is connected with spirituality. It is the link between our material and spiritual realms. When the crown chakra is open, we remember our connection to the divine truth. We remember our spiritual nature as our true essence and that we are eternal spiritual creatures.

Now imagine a sphere of violet light surrounding the top of the head. Breathe into this light. Have the intention of opening this center. Visualize this light becoming more brilliant, illuminating, expanding in all directions, out into the world and all of creation. The mantra for the seventh, or crown, chakra is the universal sound AUM, pronounced OM. As you exhale, let this sound flow from the crown of the head out into the world and all of creation.

When all the colors of the chakras blend, we create a pure white light. Now envision a ring of radiant white light beginning to encircle the crown of the head. With attention and intention, allow this light to travel down to encompass the forehead. Let this light glide down and surround the throat, embrace the heart, and encircle the belly to the base of the spine. Allow this light to radiate down the legs, journeying down to the tips of the toes. Feel yourself filled with this healing white light. Breathe in this light. Absorb this energy into your being.

Now take a slow, deep breath in and out. Be aware of how you feel in this moment both in body and mind. Take another deep breath. Feel the surface beneath you, and listen to the sounds around you. Gently move your fingers and toes. And when you feel ready, slowly open the eyes.

In Closing

The chakras have been known by healing cultures for thousands of years as one measurement of wellness. The body is a mirror of our life condition. Appreciating the human energy system is vital to understanding ourselves and our purpose. Our chakras exchange and absorb energies between the body and the physical world, as well as draw in energy from the Divine Source. Chakras govern the mental, emotional, physical, and spiritual qualities of our being. Here are a few points to remember.

- The seven major chakras manage the vital bodily functions and concerns.

- Chakra healing can be a way to help restore an imbalance, reduce the onset of illness, and promote wellness. It's important to have all of the chakras balanced and cleared of energy field disturbances.

- You can use your senses, sound, color, and spiritual practices to aid in releasing blockages.

- Once the chakras are open, energy can flow freely through the chakras.

- Caring for your physical, mental, spiritual, and energetic bodies is vital in achieving health, wellness, and a sense of wholeness.

In the next chapter, you'll learn how to manage and replenish your energy to prevent burnout and promote clarity and vitality. You will know how to create a healing environment for your living and work space.

CHAPTER 18

Energy Management

"The higher your energy level, the more efficient your body. The more efficient your body, the better you feel and the more you will use your talent to produce outstanding results."
—ANTHONY ROBBINS

As we expend energy, we need to regain energy, and we refuel it by how we live our lives. Thoughts, emotions, and behaviors either recharge or deplete our energy. Consuming large amounts of caffeine and sugar as a pick-me-up is not a substitute for adequately managing your energy. Everything covered so far in these pages has contributed to managing and maintaining your vitality. High-vibration living through meditation, eating healthy food, exercise, getting a good night's sleep, and managing emotional health all help replenish our mental, emotional, physical, and spiritual energy.

I am an advocate for energy management and timelines, not time management and deadlines. Who wants to feel the pressure of racing against the clock with the looming fear of not meeting a DEADline? Even the energy surrounding those words can feel draining. On the other hand, accomplishing a task by managing your energy and having a timetable as a guide sounds more doable and supportive. This chapter suggests various ways to practice energy management and make good use of time.

The Ultradian Healing Response

Everything in nature needs periods of rest and activity. When we get caught up in daily routines and work, we can tune out when the body needs to rest. Always on the go with no breaks deprives the body of necessary rest that can result in mental, emotional, and physical problems. How many times do you ignore signals that your energy is weakening, like yawning, hunger, restlessness, and difficulty focusing? We must observe, feel, and listen when the body needs to stop and rest.

In a study published in 2011 in the journal *Cognition*, research professor Alejandro Lleras suggests "brief mental breaks keep you focused." This activity-rest exchange is essential to refill your energy reserves, maintain clarity, and prevent burnout. In 1960, physiologist and sleep researcher Nathaniel Kleitman discovered what he calls the "basic rest-activity cycle or BRAC." Other researchers have called it ultradian rhythm. During his sleep studies, Kleitman revealed that the body goes through various rest-activity cycles of sleep throughout the night known as REM (rapid eye movement) and non-REM sleep. It was determined that these active and non-active cycles occur during our waking hours as well.

Expanding on Kleitman's research, Ernest Rossi, PhD, psychologist, and author of *The Twenty Minute Break,* coined the term *ultradian healing response*. Rossi focuses on the resting cycles the body needs throughout the day to allow the mind to rest and refocus. He breaks down the rest-activity cycle into 90 minutes of targeted activity followed by a 20-minute break to relax and recharge the mind and body.

When you begin your 90-minute activity, set a timer to help you know when to stop and rest. After 90 minutes of focused work when the mind is not as clear, stop working for 20 minutes. During your break, remove yourself from your work area and do something not work-related that will refuel you. Engage in a relaxing activity that is not physically or mentally taxing or intense. Be mindful and notice any changes in your mental or emotional state.

After you have achieved the 90 minutes of uninterrupted, concentrated work and can nurture yourself with the 20-minute break, you can now play with the times. Rossi teaches that each person needs to determine how long their cycles last and that the 90/20 rule is only a basic model. We must listen to the body's signals and know the body's needs and adjust the cycles accordingly. Recognize when you need to take a break and how much rest you need. You may need to rest after 60, 75, or 80 minutes of work and then feel fully rested after only 10 or 15 minutes. Under certain work conditions, you may only get time for 10 minutes of rest. Use that time to relax fully. Which cycle is ideal? Everyone is different. Know what works best for you by tuning in and listening to the needs of the body and mind.

Pomodoro Technique

There is an alternative approach to manage your energy and boost your productivity. The Pomodoro Technique developed by Francesco Cirillo uses 25-minute task and 5-minute break time intervals. He refers to each time interval as a Pomodoro, Italian for *tomato* because the timer he uses for this technique is a kitchen timer shaped like a tomato. I will explain a simple approach to this technique.

To begin, choose a single task you want to complete. Set a timer for 25 minutes and concentrate fully on the work without interruption. Then take a 5-minute breather. Have a healthy snack or beverage, take a walk, stretch, or close the eyes and breathe. You have completed one Pomodoro. Then either continue with the previous task or start a new one. After four Pomodoros, take a 20- to 30-minute break. See the inset on the following page.

Create Space

How does your living and work space look and feel? Our outer world (surroundings) reflects our inner world (thoughts, beliefs, and feelings).

My Experience with Rest-Activity Techniques

I have found both the ultradian healing response and the Pomodoro Technique invaluable. Which one I use depends on the task at hand. Both keep the mind fresh and the body energized, whether I apply it to my work or home tasks that require my full and undivided attention. My sessions with clients are 90 minutes, and I schedule a 30-minute break between each session. During my respite, I take 15 minutes to connect with nature, walk my dog, eat, or drink a glass of infused water, like basil or rosemary with lemon, before preparing for my next client. I find the morning hours the best time for my most important or focused work, like right now writing this book. When I'm doing any writing, my break is playing the piano. It relaxes and inspires me and helps keep my creative juices flowing.

Our surroundings mirror what is going on inside us. If your desk, office, or living areas are in complete disarray, you may feel anxious and confused. Clutter on the inside creates clutter on the outside. Everyone has experienced living with accumulated and disorganized piles of stuff. No home or work space is in perfect order all the time. When is clutter too much?

Clutter is a sign of blocked energy and can deplete your vibrancy, cause anxiety, and create sensory overload. Staying focused can be a challenge. Mess is stress. It increases cortisol, the hormone that contributes to the fight/flight/freeze response. Sifting through the clutter to find something or frantically trying to clear the space to entertain friends is a waste of time. It robs you of doing more enjoyable activities. Stagnant energy tends to collect in corners where disorganized mounds of paper or items are usually stacked. Energy needs to keep moving and flow freely.

The process of decluttering or creating space, as I like to call it, is vital. When we create space and remove the stagnation, it can feel expansive, light, and free. Set your mind on creating more space in your life. Put it on your schedule and commit to yourself to do it. Be realistic in your planning, so you feel confident in achieving your goals. Start with a smaller area of clutter. As you go through the items, give away, file away, throw away, or sell things you do not need and that don't add value to your life.

Self-Inquiry Exercise: Take inventory. Look around your home and work space. What do you notice? How does it make you feel? What areas contain clutter? Which areas are clear? Remember to check your desk area, closets, refrigerator, pantry, and under the bed. In your journal, respond to the following prompts with your thoughts and insights:

- How many areas do you need to create space?
- Which area will you clear first and when (date)? Remember, you may want to start small.
- List three more areas where you will create space.

Clearing Stagnant Energy

Have you ever needed to take a walk to clear your head? By moving your energy, you removed stagnant or stuck energy that was blocking or disrupting your creative thought processes. Similarly, our living and work spaces can have blocked energy that affects our energy fields and requires clearing.

Once you have created more space in your home or office area, how do you know if you need to dissolve any sluggish energy? Listen to the body for signs. Notice if you are feeling exhausted all of a sudden, depressed for no reason, argumentative, or you are attracting negative relationships or situations. Other times a clearing may be needed: when you move into a new home, after home construction, or after negative individuals have been in your home for an extended period.

To prepare the area, open the blinds or draperies to fill the space with light. Open the windows and doors to allow the energy to flow freely through the room(s). When clearing an entire home, you can start and finish by the front door. When clearing a single room, begin at the door leading into the room. Move around the living space in a clockwise direction to cover all areas and invite in tranquility, harmony, and prosperity. Remember to include any corners, windows, doorways, hallways, bathrooms, and closets. Throughout the clearing, have the intention of moving undesirable energy out and replacing it with pure, positive energy.

According to Ayurveda, the five elements (space, air, fire, water, and earth) link up with the five senses (hearing, smell, sight, taste, and touch). Using the five elements is an excellent way to dissolve blocked energy. Here are some suggestions:

* Space (hearing). This element is about expansion and infinite possibilities. Sound and music break up stuck energy. Move around the room playing an instrument like a drum, singing bowl, rattle, or clap your hands. You can sing or chant the sound of *Aum* (*Om*), or say a prayer. Move the sound around the room. Play your instrument three times in the corners.

* Air (touch). This element is about movement and change. Wash your hands before and after clearing to loosen and remove stagnant energy.

* Fire (sight). This element is about cultivating passion and vision. Burning white candles to remove negative energy has been used for centuries by many cultures. Use candles in glass containers during this ritual to prevent a fire. As the flame burns, it fills the space with inspiration and creativity.

- Water (taste). This element cleanses and is about flow and flexibility. When you are dispelling the energy, stay well hydrated and flush the body of any accumulation of negative energy from the space. You can shower afterward with the intention that any remaining stagnant energy surrounding you is going down the drain.

- Earth (smell). This element is about feeling grounded and secure. Smudging is an ancient practice where you burn white sage to clear a space. Light the dried herb, blow out the flame, and let the red embers burn as the smoke billows. Use a container like a large shell to collect the ash. Use your hand or a feather to fan and spread the smoke, paying particular attention to the corners. Snuff out the embers when you are finished.

How I Perform a Clearing Ritual

First, I wash my hands. Then I place a white unlit votive candle in the rooms I am going to clear. I keep a lighter in my pocket. Then starting at the front door, I play the drum, Tibetan bowl, or rattle from room to room shaking up the energy throughout the house. Next, I burn the white sage and smudge myself first. Then I proceed throughout space again, as I combine smudging and chanting. When I finish with a room, I light the candle. I continue to the next area until I reach the front door again. To complete the ritual, I douse the burning embers, blow out all the candles, drink some infused water, and rinse off in the shower.

Creating a Healing and Peaceful Environment

Once you've created and cleared energy, you've essentially created a foundation for a sacred place where you can feel nourished and secure. Are you ready to replace the old chaotic energy with calm, spacious, and soothing energy? Redesigning and filling a sacred space that promotes healing and peace is both practical and personal. Be creative in your choices. The easiest way to do this is by pleasing all of your senses. Here are some suggestions:

- Place as much emphasis on the outside area of your living space as you do with the inside. Keep the grounds attractive and clutter free.

- Create an inviting front entranceway with plants, flowers, and perhaps a fountain.

- Remove your shoes when you enter your home. The soles contain pollutants from the outside, so avoid tracking toxins throughout your home. Change into a pair of house shoes, if necessary.

- Flowers say you are worthy of love and happiness. You can go all out with full bouquets or merely place a flower in a single bud vase in your meditation area, on your desk, or any other area where you will see it often.

- Plants give off oxygen and take in the carbon dioxide. Besides bringing natural beauty into your space, they add humidity to the air and improve inside air quality.

- Fountains create a relaxing and soothing sound that can also act as white noise to cover up any unpleasant sounds. Be aware of the sounds in your environment. Recognize which sounds are nourishing and which are toxic. The body absorbs every sound it hears. Fountains also add natural humidity to the air.

- Aromatherapy uses essential oils to elicit specific physiological and psychological effects. The different aromas can de-stress, alter your mood, calm, or invigorate. Fill your home with these smells using a diffuser or a room spray.

- Create an area dedicated as your quiet place where you can meditate, read, or journal. Make it unique with soft pillows, throw blankets, and soothing colors.

- Play calming or uplifting music when you are not at home. When you return, your living space can be a welcoming and peaceful retreat.

- If possible, discourage negative, low-vibration people from spending too much time in your home. When they leave, spray one of your favorite essential oil aromas to dispel the energy.

Disconnect to Reconnect

Do you wake up and immediately check your smartphone for messages? Are you on social media all day long? Is your TV on whenever you are home? Do you use your smartphone at the dining table?

As a society, we are on energy and sensory overload. Technology bombards us. The constant smartphone, email, and internet alerts keep us continuously on alert. Being on alert is a stress response. The body and mind need a digital detox vacation to restore, recharge, and reconnect. To start, I recommend that, for at least an hour each day, you unplug yourself from your computer, smartphone, and TV. This disconnect can be the hour before bedtime or when you wake up. If it's easier, you can split it up and do a half hour in the morning and a half hour in the evening. Then increase your time to an hour both in the morning and the evening. Start and end each day in touch and in tune with your higher Self and Divine Source. You can even indulge yourself and spend an entire day away from technology and spend your time communing with nature, calling on friends, or engaging in physical activities and sports that require no electronics.

Set aside time daily to be quiet and do something relaxing that doesn't involve electronics. Here are some ideas:

- Relax in a comfortable chair or lie down, close the eyes, and release your imagination.

- Sit or walk in nature and observe the sounds, colors, movement, and fragrances.

- Take a walk with your pet.

- Watch a sunrise or sunset.

- Meditate and reconnect with your soul.

YOUR TURN FOR SELF-DISCOVERY

As you review this chapter, notice in what way the information changed your way of thinking about how you manage your energy. Observe the effects energy has on your living or work space.

Self-Inquiry Exercise: Choose two separate days to apply each of the energy-management techniques you learned in this chapter. You can choose any task that requires your focus either at work or home. In your journal, respond to the following prompts with your thoughts and insights:

- Ultradian Healing Response: What single task(s) did you choose? How did you feel after 90-minute focused tasks? Were you able to know when the body and mind needed to rest, and what signs could you identify? How did you feel after a 20-minute breather?

- Pomodoro Technique: What single task(s) did you choose? How did you feel with 25 minutes of focused tasks followed by 5-minute pauses? How many Pomodoros did you do before taking a 20-minute break? How did you feel after a 20-minute respite?

- Do you think either of these techniques could be helpful to you? If yes, which approach and how would it benefit you?
- As you take a more in-depth look inside, can you discern the underlying reasons for the clutter in your space?
- Share your experience for each of the positive energy practices: clearing negative energy in your living or work space, create a healing and peaceful environment, and disconnect to reconnect.

In Closing

Using and conserving our energy in a health-promoting way is essential for wellness. The following are seven main points to remember:

- It's crucial to know the signs of mental, emotional, and physical fatigue and stress. Knowing when to take a break from tasks helps you from depleting your energy reserves.
- Aligning with your basic rest-activity cycle aids in keeping your biological rhythms in balance and the mind and body healthier.
- Clutter is negative energy that blocks the flow of life-affirming energy. Living in clutter can make you feel anxious, tired, or depressed.
- Decluttering your living or work space creates space and allows positive energy to flow naturally without interruption. It's beneficial to help elevate your life by replacing clutter with flowing and uplifting energy.

- As significant as it is to take rest breaks from work, it's equally as important to schedule time out from smartphones, computers, tablets, and TV.

- Being on alert all your waking hours and answering your smartphone and emails can trigger the fight/flight/freeze response.

- Daily digital detoxing and taking breaks from electronic devices will help restore your energy. It's also an excellent mental health practice, which is vital nowadays.

The next two chapters will explore how sound and music are healing forces. You will learn how to tune in to your environment and use music in your everyday life to support your overall well-being.

CHAPTER 19

Healing Mysteries of Sound and Music: Part I

"The medicine of the future will be music and sound."
—EDGAR CAYCE

Have you ever tapped your foot or bobbed your head while listening to music? Has listening to music ever brought you to tears or raised your skin with goosebumps as a rippling wave of sensations flowed through you? Do you remember hearing a song that brought back memories? Do the sounds of the ocean or the song of birds relax you? Sound and music affect us.

Music has been feeding my soul for as long as I can remember. As a young child, I recall lying under our grand piano listening to my parents play and feel the music pour over me. I was already experiencing the healing mysteries of sound and music and the powerful effect on the body, mind, and spirit. Now, I would like to share with you simple ways you can benefit. These next two chapters are a mere prelude to a symphony I can compose about the vast topic of healing with music and sound. My focus is on how to lower stress, promote relaxation, and facilitate a sense of well-being.

Sound and music have been used in healing cultures throughout the ages. Ancient philosophers like Pythagoras, Plato, and Aristotle recognized its importance in healing. In our modern world, we use sound and music terms to describe health—being of sound mind and body, feeling upbeat, getting in tune, being in sync, composing yourself, and being in harmony.

Sound Body

The physical body is composed of sound. Every system in the body has its own cycle, rhythm, and pulse. Think of the body as an orchestra and each cell and organ is a finely tuned instrument vibrating with its own particular frequency or pitch. For the sounds to be harmonious, each instrument or cell must be in tune with the other instruments or cells. When an instrument is out of tune, it can affect the entire orchestra, and a discordant sound emerges. When our cells are not vibrating in tune, it affects the whole body. There is a feeling of dis-easement in the body, and we are no longer in harmony. All the vibratory components of our bodies need to be in tune and in sync with each other. In his book, *Sounds of Healing,* Mitchell Gaynor, MD, an oncologist, explains, "You can look at disease as a form of disharmony. And there's no organ system in the body that's not affected by sound and music and vibration." Our role as the conductor of our internal symphony is to orchestrate harmony.

Principles of Sound

We are surrounded by sound twenty-four hours a day, so it's helpful to know more about how it affects us and our health. When using sound and music to heal, we look at the phenomenon of resonance, the theory of entrainment, and the science of cymatics to understand how the sound vibrations that surround us affect us. Let's look at the principles of sound as it relates to wellness.

Sympathetic Resonance

When we say we resonate with something or someone, what does that mean? Resonance is when one energy field can alter other energy fields. Sympathetic resonance is when a vibrating object causes another vibrating object that has the same tonal frequency to vibrate. When you hear rumbling thunder, you may feel objects in your house vibrating or moving. The thunder resonates and sends out sound waves that find other resonating objects of the same matching tonal frequency, resulting in that object also vibrating. The items are vibrating together in sympathy or agreement with the thunder. An example of human resonance is when two people feel connected. They are in harmony and share a harmonic likeness, as they are in sync and are beating to the same rhythmic pulse.

Resonance is vital for our health and well-being. It shifts energy. When we encounter an illness, our natural resonance is replaced with dissonance. We can use sound and music to restore the body's fundamental frequencies and reestablish our connection with our true essence to a more harmonious state. Sympathetic resonance is also necessary between a client and a healer because for healing to occur, resonance must be created.

Entrainment

The principle of entrainment was discovered by Dutch scientist and inventor of the pendulum clock, Christiaan Huygens, in 1665. In his experiment, he hung a group of pendulum clocks on a wall in a room with all the pendulums swinging at different rates. After a day or two, he found that all the pendulums were synchronized and swaying at the same speed. The science of entrainment states that when two nearby vibrating or oscillating bodies come together, they merge and synchronize to the stronger vibration and vibrate as one in harmony. Birds flying together in a synchronized and rhythmic pattern is entrainment. You are entraining with the music when you dance and move your feet in time to the beat of the music. Next time you are at a performance, listen to how the audience's clapping comes together in unison. We can apply this law to create changes in the body, mind, and emotions.

Cymatics

Sound waves create visible patterns and can affect and rearrange physical matter. Cymatics is the study of sound waves made visible. When an opera singer matches the same musical pitch and resonant frequency of the glass, the air molecules around the glass vibrate as well. As the singer increases the volume, the vibrations of the air particles also intensify to the point where the glass can no longer remain intact, and the glass shatters. Knowing this, imagine what sound can do to the body. This knowledge has crossed over into the medical field. A procedure known as lithotripsy uses ultrasound shock waves to break up kidney stones, making it easier for the body to pass the smaller particles of stone through the urine. Sound waves are also used in the treatment of cataracts.

Being Mindful of Sound

Sounds can soothe and heal or irritate and cause harm. They can promote health with a feeling of well-being or raise our stress levels and make us ill. Our bodies are continually resonating and entraining with the sounds in our environment. We may not even be aware of how the body is reacting to these sounds. The mind can ignore the surrounding sounds, yet the body is still affected by them because our ears cannot be turned off.

When we are mindful of our surroundings, we can tune in to the many pleasant and unpleasant sound waves influencing the body, mind, and emotions. We are alerted with rings, beeps, and alarms from our electronic devices. Wind moving through the trees, running water, TV, traffic, loud talking, and office noise all emit vibrations and can be perceived as enjoyable or upsetting. Unpleasant sounds can trigger our fight/flight/freeze response and contribute to tension, irritability, anxiety, headaches, poor digestion, and sleep disturbances.

I invite you to do an exercise with me right now. Close the eyes and tune in to your environment. How many background sounds do you hear both near and far? Which sounds are pleasing or unpleasant to you? As I sit here writing, I hear the beautiful song of mockingbirds outside my window. I notice the hum of the air-conditioning unit. The water fountain's trickling sound feels relaxing. I listen to my fingers clicking away at the computer keyboard. There is a soft knock coming from the ceiling. Way off in the distance, I hear a dog barking and lawn mowers. These are some of the sounds that become my surrounding soundscape, my landscape of sounds. I have learned how to hear and accept both soothing and irritating sounds. It is the musical backdrop of my life.

How to Alter Sound

Some sounds can get on your nerves. When we encounter an annoying sound, we can learn to accept it, so it does not negatively affect us. We can move from resisting the noise to resonating with it. Here are four ways to alter your perception of the sounds:

- Acknowledge the sound and then redirect your focus to what you were doing.
- Play with the sound until it no longer bothers you. Imitate it with your voice or add your own rhythmic patterns to make the noise more interesting.
- As you become aware of the sound, use your imagination, and take a 2-minute mini-vacation. Go to your relaxing, happy place. Develop the scene using your five senses so you feel like you are really there. What do you hear, see, touch, smell, and taste? As you become calmer, notice the annoying sounds fade into the background.

❖ Listen to the sound mindfully to let go of the emotional stress response. Notice where the annoying sound is resonating in the body. Imagine relaxing this area with the breath as you release the emotional charge underlying your reaction. Then tune in to nature sounds or relaxing music to compose a new soundscape. No wonder many homes have water fountains, fireplaces, and wind chimes as part of a healing decor.

What Is Sound Healing?

Sound healing is the intentional and therapeutic use of sound frequencies or vibrations to improve physical, mental, and emotional health and bring about a state of harmony, healing, and sense of well-being. The vibratory components of the body need to be in tune and in sync with one another to experience and maintain health. As Mitch Gaynor, MD, professed in his book, *The Healing Power of Sound: Recovery from Life-Threatening Illness Using Sound, Voice, and Music*, "Sound can redress imbalances on every level of physiologic functioning and can play a positive role in the treatment of virtually any disease." It can help quiet the mind, open our consciousness, and connect us with our soul. Drums, rattles, gongs, singing bowls, Tibetan bowls, the voice, Native American flute, harp, and didgeridoos are some instruments used to heal through sound.

Tama-Do Sound Therapy

In 1981, Fabien Maman, a French musician/composer, acupuncturist, author and researcher, conducted cellular biology experiments at the University of Jussieu in Paris. His revolutionary research revealed the effect of sound on human cells and the subtle energy fields. His findings showed that through a specific progression of musical sounds, healthy cells became strengthened and revitalized, and cancer cells exploded. His further research included the link between the cells and the soul. In his book *The Tao of Sound*, Maman teaches, "When scientific research, spiritual practice, and artistic expression work together, heaven and earth are in resonance. This is the vibratory promise that is the gift of our musical universe."

In 1987, Maman formed the Tama-Do (way of the soul) Academy, committed to the development of human consciousness. His research and teachings to balance the physical body, chakras, and subtle energy fields credited him as the founding father of vibrational sound therapy. Ten years earlier, he created the system of using tuning forks tuned to the twelve notes of the musical scale in place of needles on acupuncture points on the body. The Tama-Do practices he teaches use sound, colored silks and light, and color essences to move energy, reestablish harmony, and aid the body in the recovery of its own balance in health. The techniques help reduce physical and emotional stress and anxiety, relieve discomfort, promote inner peace, and connect you with your inner light.

After years of study with Fabien Maman, I have been applying these sophisticated and delicate Tama-Do protocols with remarkable results. Immediately following a session, clients have reported feeling "calm and hopeful," "zero stress," "incredible like I was just born," "no more back pain," "like I've been transported to cloud nine," "deeply relaxed and lighter," "peaceful and whole," and "no pain like I had an emotional release."

Another practice is Tama-Do Sound Harmonization®—*Harmonizing the Chakras and Energy Fields (Aura) with acoustic instruments and elemental sounds.* Using instruments representing the five elements of Nature (earth, water, wood, fire, and air), it can clear energetic blockages so that we can find a place of stillness within ourselves. After a session, participants shared, "the sounds were mesmerizing" and "I feel lighter, calm, and relaxed."

Terres Unsoeld, Master Teacher of Tama-Do Academy, affirms, "This is a marvelous opportunity to experience the subtle and profound effects of acoustic sound in the aura to harmonize the body, mind and spirit—as created by Fabien Maman, the Founding Father of vibrational sound therapy."

Vocal Toning

The voice is the most potent readily available healing instrument. What sound would you make if you burned yourself, stubbed your toe, or needed to clear your throat? The body is continuously making sound, as we breathe, yawn, cry, laugh, sigh, sneeze, cough, or make any other bodily function noises. We naturally make toning sounds to release energy and bring the body back in tune. I learned the benefits of natural vocal sounds in 1973 after reading Laurel Elizabeth Keyes's book, *Toning: The Creative Power of the Voice*. Keyes states, "The purpose of all toning is to restore the vibratory pattern of the body to its perfect electromagnetic field so that it will function in harmony with itself."

Toning is a vibrational therapy where we make vocal sounds that are void of melody, rhythm, or words. Because there are no words to think about, it allows us to experience our heart and soul. It uses repeated drawn-out vowel sounds that are held to the end of an exhale. There is no right or wrong way to tone, and any sound you produce is the correct one for you at that moment. The left brain and ego self may want to judge and say it is not a beautiful sound. Ignore that internal message. The right brain and body will tune in and feel the natural and immediate release and centering effect. Focus on what the vibration you are producing feels like rather than on how it sounds.

The toning process teaches us how to release natural vocal sounds to achieve a feeling of balance and harmony. Daily toning can help oxygenate the blood, improve breath flow and posture, boost the immune system, and energize the body. It helps release tension, negative energy, bottled-up emotions, and stress. Toning removes blocked energy or redirects it to where it is needed in the body.

Toning is usually done in private or in a retreat setting. The following is one way to tone using the *Ooo, Oh, Ah,* and *Eee* vowel sounds. As you tone each vowel, feel and connect with your rhythm. Be aware of the different shapes and positions of the mouth and tongue with each vowel. Engage the navel area to access more air and channel your energy. Pull the navel inward and up to control the slow and steady release of the breath. If the navel area and third chakra are weak, it can disrupt our power. As we express ourselves through the voice, we can connect with, develop, and strengthen our authentic sound. Tone each vowel for 3 to 5 minutes or until you feel a pleasant and subtle energy shift. Toning in the morning following your meditation sets your tone for the day.

* As a warm-up, bounce up and down to stimulate the lymphatic system and get the blood flowing. Shake the whole body. Roll the shoulders forward and backward three times each. Stretch the arms up and reach upward and then relax.

* To begin, either stand straight with feet hip-width apart with knees loose or sit erect in a chair.

* Close the eyes to keep your awareness inward. Relax the jaw. You can warm up the voice with a few low-sounding groans or deep sighs. Breathe in through the nose and allow the body to naturally move or rock as you release with sound on the exhale.

* Inhale and, as you exhale slowly, start toning the *Ooo* sound (as in true). Using a low, deep tone, feel any tension, stress, or pain being drained out of the body through the feet. When you are finished, open the eyes and notice what you are feeling.

* Inhale and, as you exhale slowly, start toning the *Oh* sound. Feel the sound resonating within the navel as its vibration empowers you. When you are finished, open the eyes and notice what you are feeling.

* Inhale and, as you exhale slowly, start toning the *Ah* sound. Imagine the heart chakra opening and the chest relaxing. Feel the vibration radiating from the heart outward. When you are finished, open the eyes and notice what you are feeling.

- Inhale and, as you exhale slowly, start toning the *Eee* sound. Using a higher pitch, imagine this sound emanating outward from the crown of the head. As the vibrations create more space, feel a sense of clarity. When you are finished, open the eyes and notice what you are feeling.
- End with a few deep breaths in and sigh as you breathe out.

Try This: Releasing Pain

We have an innate response to cry, say "ouch," or moan when feeling pain. We can intentionally use sound to ease the pain. As you are experiencing pain, locate that pain in the body. Then, make a vocal sound that matches the pain to help release it. You are putting a voice to that pain. Feel free to moan or groan or use different vowel sounds with low or high pitches. You may tone for 5 to 10 minutes or for as long as you feel is necessary. Observe the before and after effects in the physical, mental, and emotional bodies.

Peggy's Story

I first met Peggy at my center in St. John in 2007. She had a high-pressured leadership position at work, and her job-related fears seemed to be ruling her life. She was looking for a deeper meaning for her life. She also expressed her anxieties about turning forty. She stated that her stress level was 11 on a scale from 1 to 10, with weekly panic attacks and problems sleeping. She desired to change how she lived her life. Peggy and I co-created her weeklong wellness retreat plan that started with meditation.

Next, she arrived at her Tama-Do vibrational sound and color healing session. When I started using the tuning forks on the body, she began crying and releasing pent-up emotional energy. I encouraged her to continue to let go, and she immediately burst into wailing sounds. I toned aloud with her in support. Together we groaned and moaned, as I made dissonant tones to help her release the pain. When her vocal tones shifted, I moved to more harmonious sounds. Her toning ebbed and flowed for half an hour and diminished into soft whimpering. Then, I used the Tama-Do protocols to restore harmony. At one point, she said she saw herself as a child lying in the grass looking up at the willow tree she used to climb as a kid. A sense of euphoria and freedom came over her. She started giggling.

Afterward, we discussed the healing that took place. Peggy said that she felt like a ton of bricks had dropped from her shoulders. My toning with her gave her the permission she needed to surrender and let go. She returned to that uninhibited expression and freedom to spontaneously make sounds that she remembered making as a child. At the end of the retreat, she said she felt "happy and peaceful." She believed she "felt and saw the colors of her soul." We hugged goodbye as she began to cry with joy. She said she was starting to believe that a more meaningful life was possible.

Three months later, I received an email from Peggy. "Cannot wait to share with you dramatic results I have felt since I left your center! Better sleep all around, less tension/nervousness, better clarity, and more! I have not had a panic attack in these past three months. Excited about the prospect of even better benefits. Still doing plan. Been toning and doing humming breath. Feels good. Thanks for caring."

Over the years, Peggy continues to work with me in private one-on-one retreats. In the past year, she was coming to an exciting major turning point in her life. The focus of her most recent retreat was to "clear old stuck energy" before starting her new career adventure. Her retreat included three Tama-Do sessions, coaching, and mentoring. After her Tama-Do sessions, she said, "My back totally opened, and there's no pain. I feel like I was transported to another place. I feel peaceful, contemplative, and refreshed like coming out of a deep sleep. I'm resolved in moving forward. I feel great."

YOUR TURN FOR SELF-DISCOVERY

I hope you now have a better understanding of we are affected by sound. Sounds nourish or deplete the body. Not only do we create a physical body by the food we ingest, but we also create a body by the sounds we absorb.

Self-Inquiry Exercise: For a day, pay attention to all the sounds entering the body, starting with your alarm clock if you use one. Keep a small pad with you and make a running list of the sounds throughout the day. Aim to record at least twenty sounds. After you listen to the sound, place a P next to the sound if you felt it was pleasing and nourishing. Place a U next to the sound if you felt it was unpleasant and depleting. Be aware of how the body and mind reacted. Note if the body responded favorably or adversely to each sound you noticed. In your journal, respond to the following prompts with your thoughts and insights:

- ❖ Review How to Alter Sound on page 213. Which of the four practices helped you deal with any unpleasant sounds in your environment?

- ❖ In what ways can you add nourishing sounds in your home and work space?

- What activities can you incorporate into your life to absorb more sounds of nature?
- Review the section Vocal Toning on page 216. Practice toning and write about your experience and any physical sensations before, during, and after.

In Closing

More and more people are exploring the science behind energy and vibrational healing as a viable approach to support health and wellness. It's helpful to recognize the body's response to both pleasing and unpleasant sounds. We can use the vibrations of natural sounds, instruments, tuning forks, and vocal toning to counteract the effects of stress and maximize the body's ability to heal. Key points to remember:

- The physical body is composed of sound.
- Your cells and organs need to be vibrating together in harmony to balance and restore the body.
- The principles of resonance, entrainment, and cymatics are used in healing.
- It is possible to alter your perception of annoying sounds.
- Balance your environment with sounds of nature.
- Tuning fork practices help unblock stuck energy and restore harmony in the body, mind, and soul.
- Toning is a way to release tension, energize the body, and open the throat chakra to strengthen your voice in life.

The next chapter shares how music can be used to shift the body's energy to cultivate wellness. It can help reduce stress, induce relaxation, and heal the physical, mental, emotional, and spiritual bodies.

CHAPTER 20

Healing Mysteries of Sound and Music: Part II

"Music is a moral law. It gives soul to the universe, wings to the mind, flight to the imagination, and charm and gaiety to life and to everything."

—PLATO

Next time you watch a scary movie or a tearjerker, turn off the sound. Notice the difference in your emotional and physical reactions when there is no music playing. The movie is not as scary or emotionally moving. Then turn the sound back on and feel the effects of the music. Music can affect the body, stimulate emotions, and alter your mood. It can relax, calm, inspire, and energize. It can give us goose bumps, send shivers up our spine, and suspend us in time. Music speaks to us and music can speak for us. It can help us celebrate good times and get us through times of crisis. It can bring people together for a common purpose. We see this at sporting events, birthday celebrations, campfires, army drills, weddings, religious ceremonies, and healing rituals.

Even though music can bring people together as one, each person responds to music individually. We also develop associations with music. For instance, one person hears a song that reminds them of a first date, and it brings a smile to their face. Another person hearing the same song may feel sad because they associate that song with an unpleasant incident. One type of music may be relaxing to one person while it may produce stress in someone else. The comparisons here are virtually endless because everyone has an individual experience when they hear a piece of music.

In this chapter, we'll delve into the healing power of music. We will explore music therapy and the impact music has in medicine and the healing arts. You will learn how to use music for relaxation, listen to music consciously, and create a personalized healing music library.

Music Therapy

There is an overlay between sound healing and music therapy. As defined by the American Music Therapy Association, "Music Therapy is the clinical and evidence-based use of music interventions . . . to address the physical, emotional, cognitive, and social needs of individuals." Emphasis is on the therapeutic relationship within the systematic use of music. It focuses on listening to or making music individually or within a group setting with specific goals in mind. Music therapy is an extension of sound healing.

In Rehabilitation Medicine

In the early 1980s, I created music therapy programs for the children and adults at Rusk Institute for Rehabilitation Medicine under the auspices of the hospital auxiliary headed by Mrs. Ruth Frost. The JC Penny and Gimbel families funded the program. I brought music into mainstream medicine as a valuable addition to patient care. Dr. Rusk took a personal and active interest in what was considered back then to be an innovative program.

The physical injuries and disabilities the patients were challenged with covered a wide range of diagnoses. The music therapy program included visualization and guided meditation set to classical music to relax and ease pain, making sounds like *ahh* and yoga breathing practices to reduce stress and anxiety and increase lung capacity. Group drumming and creative music making was a hit with the children. Every child had an important part, even if it was to play just one note on an instrument. They were excited to be a part of the whole. Watching how thrilled they were to perform for their families and hospital staff was emotionally moving. The medical team commented on how music therapy helped improve the patients' motor skills and movement, and enhanced self-confidence, self-esteem, and quality of life.

With Hospitalized Patients

Back in the seventies, when I was a nurse in the hospital, I would introduce healing practices to patients during my evening medication rounds. If the person was in pain, anxious, or depressed, I had them either use toning as a release or do the bumblebee humming breath (see page 125) to settle them down. I used visualizations or guided meditations to help ease their fear, tension, and discomfort. Afterward, I was amazed that those patients asked for pain and sleep medications much less frequently. Now, studies have shown music can be as effective as 7 mg of diazepam (Valium) in reducing anxiety.

Once while I was still a nursing student, a member of the nursing staff asked me to come to the hospital because one of my elderly male patients was going to pass soon and was a little agitated. She said she used to watch me sing with him and thought it would be nice if I were there since he had no family. I grabbed my guitar and went. When I arrived, he was semiconscious. I sang to him on and off that entire evening, and he settled down. Later, as I softly sang his favorite song, "The Lord Is My Shepherd," he gently passed away with a peaceful look on his face. This experience forever changed me and opened my eyes to the impact of music on the soul.

This next story is about my mother, who was hospitalized for a bleeding stomach ulcer. She survived the surgery. Unexpectedly after multiple poor medical judgments, she had a major stroke and was in a comatose state. After we removed her breathing tube, she was breathing on her own for a while. As her vital signs slowed down dramatically, we knew she was nearing her passage. I decided to sing "Amazing Grace" to her. My husband, my father, and I were surprised when her blood pressure and heart rate suddenly increased as I sang to her. She heard me. That afternoon, she passed. Even when her brain was severely damaged, the music touched her soul, and the body responded to the music. That moment will be forever in my heart and soul.

Music and the Healing Arts

Music has been an integral part of my life since I was five years old. However, it wasn't until age twenty-five that I learned the significance and impact of music and movement on a child's physical, mental, and emotional development and well-being. I discovered the same held true for adults. No matter what age, sound/music is a universal language that speaks volumes.

For over thirty years, I also worked with socially disadvantaged, underserved, and disabled children using the healing arts and Carl Orff's approach in music therapy. Orff was a German composer best known for his operas and innovations in elemental education in music and creative movement in the 1930s. The Orff developmental and therapeutic process uses music, speech and song, sounds, creative movement, and drama for the totality of expression. Rhythm is seen as a basic form of expression and communication. Middle, elementary, and preschool children would play various instruments and create ensembles that required cooperation, interaction, and an open imagination. I would use the movement component to encourage them to release inhibitions, build confidence, and express themselves. The music guided them to dance and act out empowering stories about their inner and outer worlds.

The children were provided with opportunities for nonverbal expression of emotions, critical thinking, and the release of tension and frustration while enhancing self-worth and self-esteem. It was beautiful to observe how they connected with their inner song while becoming the music they created or heard and felt. For many of the children, their problems and pressures dissolved in those moments. In its place were joy and a sense of accomplishment. I, too, felt a sense of fulfillment watching the therapeutic potential of music and the arts with every child to promote healing, coping, harmony, and wellness.

Health Benefits of Music

There are numerous studies and research on the effectiveness of music on health, healing, and wellness. This healing art is beneficial in helping individuals to:

- Manage physical and mental stress
- Relieve pain and discomfort
- Release muscular tension
- Lower resting heart rate
- Lower blood pressure
- Free emotional pain
- Promote relaxation
- Reduce depression
- Improve memory
- Ease anxiety
- Elevate mood
- Induce sleep

Music can also transcend ordinary states of consciousness. The logical thinking mind is limiting. When we enter into a deeper state of awareness, we tap into new possibilities and a powerful potential for healing. This is evident when we listen to a piece of music and feel like we traveled to another place and returned feeling different. Our unique experience was transformative.

Music Anatomy 101

Human beings are musical beings. Our heartbeat, brain waves, breathing, and voice are all rhythmic. So it makes sense that we would respond to music. Five elements of music are beat, rhythm, melody, harmony, and tonal quality. When we listen to music, we feel the beat and connect with the pulse of life. We feel the different rhythms that get the heart pumping, feet and body moving, and awakens our insides.

Melody is a sequence of individual musical notes that tell a story. Each note or tone has a pitch or frequency. Harmony is combining notes at the same time to complement the melody. Leonardo da Vinci believed that "our soul is composed of harmony." I agree that harmonies resonate with our soul and touch upon our emotions.

Now let's look at tonal quality. Do you like listening to certain instruments over others? Perhaps you prefer the sound of a violin over a cello or bass. Maybe you favor the sound of the French horn over the trumpet or tuba. The saxophone may appeal to you more than say the flute, oboe, or clarinet. Each instrument has a unique tonal quality, or timbre (pronounced *tamber*). It's what makes one instrument sound different from another when they are both playing the same pitch and loudness. It has to do with the way it is played. The same melodies when played on a flute, oboe, or piano will sound and feel different and evoke different emotions. Some words used to describe a sound's timbre are *warm, smooth, full, light, sharp, bright, dark,* and *brassy*.

The sounds in our environment also have distinct timbres. On a recent walk in nature, I observed birds singing the same imprinted song sounding completely different and I favored and resonated with one particular bird's sound. Each musician and singer has a *sound* they develop with their instrument. It's helpful to have a basic understanding of the elements of music and know why we like a piece that can affect us so deeply, and the qualities that determine our choices.

Music as Medicine

A key to healing is relaxation, and music has the power to bring about this desired state. But what type of music is considered relaxing? Relaxing music decreases the heart and breathing rates, calms the mind and nervous system, and shifts regular waking beta brain waves to quieting alpha waves. Personal taste in music also plays a part in which type of music will relax you. As far as selecting music, you already know music pieces that relax you. However, be aware that some of the music you might already be familiar with may not be physically relaxing because you have positive or negative associations and memories linked to that music. Avoid using these selections. So when choosing music, consider the type of music you like and also consider introducing selections that you aren't intimately familiar with. You may also pick songs with lyrics as long as they fit the following criteria and the lyrics encourage relaxation.

Here are the seven components to consider when choosing music for relaxation:

1. Slow, steady tempo
2. Simple smooth and flowing melodies
3. Simple harmonies
4. Soft dynamics
5. Lack of strong rhythmic components
6. Lack of sudden loud outbursts
7. Gradual predictable changes

When it comes to music as medicine, we can use the concept of entrainment (see page 211) to reduce stress, lower heart rate, and facilitate relaxation. In choosing musical selections, take into account the tempo or beats per minute (bpm). When we listen to music written between 50 and 70 bpm, the heart rate matches and entrains with that resting heart rate rhythm. On the other hand, if you listen to rock music written between 90 and 120 bpm, your heart rate will increase. Have you ever gone to a rock concert and felt either invigorated or totally exhausted afterward? Your heart entrained with the music.

Much of baroque music like Bach, Mozart, and Vivaldi was composed at around 60 bpm. To feel the full effects and benefits of relaxing music, I recommend listening for at least 30 minutes every day. There are many musical selections and popular songs at around 60 beats per minute. Here is a sampling:

COMPOSER	SELECTION
Anugama	Shamanic Dream
Bach	Air on the G String
Chopin	"Raindrop" Prelude Op. 28 No. 15
Beethoven	Moonlight Sonata
Debussy	Clair de Lune
Holst	Venus
Mozart	Eine Kleine Nachtmusik
Pachelbel	Canon in D
Paul Winter	Common Ground
Satie	Gymnopedie No. 1
Vivaldi	Largo from "Winter" from the Four Seasons

You may also use nonclassical music like slow jazz, music for meditation, Native America and Celtic music, or recordings of the sounds of the ocean and nature. You can choose music with lyrics as long as you feel the words are comforting and relaxing. Another option is listening to ambient music that does not focus on structured melodies and rhythm. English musician Brian Eno was the first to coin the term ambient music. In this genre of music, the waves of music continuously flow in smooth, repetitive, and layered patterns to promote a sense of calmness. Eno's 1978 composition, Ambient 1: Music for Airports, was one of the music selections I used back then for relaxation. I felt its repetitive motifs to be hypnotic and soothing.

Match Your Mood First

If you are hyperactive and very stressed and want to relax, listening to slow music may not be the initial way to go. The body is not ready to synchronize and match that beat and rhythm, and your mood. The transition needs to be gradual. Start by listening to faster music that mirrors your energy or stress level, then gradually decrease to a slower tempo piece. In music therapy, this rule is known as the Iso-principle. Authors Davis, PhD, Gfeller, PhD, and Thuat, PhD, in *An Introduction to Music Therapy Theory and Practice,* describe it as "a technique by which music is matched with the mood of a client, then gradually altered to affect the desired mood state." Music therapist, Janalea Hoffman composed music with this in mind. Her 62-minute pieces entitled Deep Daydreams and Musical Biofeedback II from her Rhythmic Medicine Series begin at 80 bpm and slow to 50 bpm. Her music eases you into relaxation.

My Music Prescription

The great composers of the baroque, classical, romantic, and impressionistic periods were divinely inspired. Their music invites the awakening of our consciousness, as we appreciate their mystical qualities. To quote Ludwig van Beethoven, "Music is the mediator between the life of the senses and the life of the spirit." As the story goes, Mozart heard his music completed before he ever wrote a note on paper. Where did it originate from? How was he able to hear the music? These questions remain a mystery.

Music is a powerful healing force. During my recovery from surgery after my near-death experience, I added music therapy to my healing process. My music prescription included listening to specific selections in classical music and Gregorian chants, depending on how I was feeling. As I listened to these and other pieces, the music transported me to another place and time where I was free of pain with no fears. I was in a peaceful and content state.

Listening to Beethoven's Piano Concerto No. 5 (Emperor) "Adagio" filled me with hope and serenity. When I needed a pick-me-up, I listened to the Bach Brandenburg Concertos to feel light, whimsical, and cheerful. I felt childlike and free. One of my favorite pieces is Albinoni's Adagio. I connected with its sweet melancholic melody to help me release heartfelt emotions and soothe my soul. There are parts where the harmony changes and moves me to tears and joy at the same time. When I wanted to go beyond ordinary states of consciousness, I chose the music of Saint Hildegard von Bingen: A Feather on the Breath of God. Hildegard (1098-1179) was a visionary nun, composer, doctor, mystic, and poet. As I played her Gregorian chant music, I surrendered into deep contemplation and felt a sense of sacredness, solace, and divine connection.

The Art of Conscious Music Listening

Sound becomes music through conscious listening and interpreting what we hear. Listening to music is a spiritual art and not a cognitive process. The body absorbs the sounds that are felt by the heart and soul. We refrain from listening with a critical or analytical ear and listen with the whole body. This shift moves our attention away from the head and our mind into the heart, emotions, and our entire being. We move from the logical left brain to the right creative and artistic brain.

Conscious listening encourages us to be present and to hear everything that is happening inside the music. It is a full sensory experience. It can tap into memories, alter mood, release and regulate emotions, and facilitate relaxation. Music can stimulate our imagination and carry us to fantasy worlds. Research shows that listening to pleasing music decreases cortisol levels, increases oxytocin, and releases dopamine, a neurotransmitter that helps regulate our emotional responses. The brain interprets the sounds as a rewarding experience resulting in the sense of euphoria.

How to Listen

Choose a peaceful place that is free of distractions. Turn off your phone. Find a comfortable seated or reclining position. Take a few relaxing breaths before you begin listening. Close the eyes as you place your full attention on the music. If you notice your attention drift away from the music to thoughts about work, issues, or responsibilities, gently guide your awareness back to the music. Let your imagination and emotions be free to explore and be led by the music. Be open to receiving messages from your inner wisdom as music can connect you with your heart consciousness. You can listen to all the instruments collectively or imagine you are one of the instruments as you follow its path. It's your choice.

When we listen mindfully, these are some of the underlying questions that await our discovery:

- What are the different rhythms and tempos?
- How does the melody flow, and where does it go?

- Do you notice any changes in your breathing pattern?
- Is the body responding with physical sensations?
- When do various instruments enter and leave?
- Are there loud and soft dynamics?
- What harmonies are present?
- Is there a shift in your emotions or mood?
- What do you like about the music you heard and felt?
- Do you have a favorite part?
- What image or journey comes to mind?

Music and Art

Another approach to mindful listening is bringing music and art together. As you listen, use pastels or crayons and draw what you hear or images the music conjures up. Let the music be the leader, the conductor. Allow yourself to go inside the music. Use an array of colors, shapes, and patterns to express how the music makes you feel. There is no right or wrong way. Let your creativity flow.

Create Your Healing Playlist Library

You can create music playlists specifically to relax, energize, elevate, or change your mood. Choose from the music you already own because you know it's music you prefer. If you are undecided, explore different musical genres that convey your feelings. Here is a list of twenty-eight categories:

• Ambient	• Baroque	• Celtic
• African	• Bluegrass	• Chant
• Ballads	• Blues	• Classical

- Country
- Disco
- Folk
- Gospel
- Heavy Metal
- Hip Hop
- Instrumental
- Jazz
- Musical Theater
- New Age
- Opera
- Pop
- Rap
- Reggae
- Religious
- Rhythm and Blues
- Rock
- Soundtracks
- World Music

Decide on what moods you want to evoke such as upbeat, energetic, calm, loving, peaceful, or uplifted. Choose six to eight music selections for each intended mood. Pick out the pieces when you are in the desired state. When you are relaxed, find music selections you feel are relaxing. You may want to review the section on Music as Medicine (see page 228). When you are ready to wind down for the day, choose music that you think will induce sleep. When you are upbeat and feeling happy, choose music that mirrors that feeling, and so on. Find music that matches how you want to feel. Then select a program where you can store your song lists for easy access.

You can also create playlists for frustration and anger, as one of my clients demonstrated. She was having a challenge at work. Annoyed that she was unfairly treated and had to abide by different rules than the men, she came up with her song list. A few of the songs were "Take This Job and Shove It" by Johnny Paycheck, "9 to 5" by Dolly Parton, and "Bad" by U2. Two months later, she quit her job and found new employment at a firm she enjoys and where she feels respected.

Tune Your Day

Music can help you be calm, relaxed, or invigorated. Here are five tips that may enhance your daily activities.

- As you're ready in the morning, listen either to calming sounds and music to feel centered or upbeat music to energize you.

- When you're walking or jogging, find music that's going to match the tempo of your walking or running steps.

- During meals, decrease stress hormones and aid your digestion with relaxing music.

- While you are working, play classical music like Bach or Mozart to boost creativity and productivity while maintaining a sense of calm.

- In the evening hours, set the mood for intimacy or wind down with ambient or 60 bpm music.

Name That Tune

When was the last time you sang your heart out? How do you feel when you sing along with the car radio? Were you encouraged to sing as a child? Perhaps you were convinced otherwise by an adult. If you can speak, you can sing. Singing is an innate ability. Young children can be heard spontaneously humming and singing songs or nonsense syllables like *la-la-la* or *bah-bah-bah*. We are music and each of us has a song to sing.

Research reveals that singing helps lower cortisol, reduce stress and anxiety, elevate mood, encourage relaxation, and promote a feeling of happiness. Letting your voice ring out in song activates the creative and intuitive right side of the brain. It helps balance the logical and information gathering left brain that is continuously processing. So, uplift yourself and sing the songs you love like a child with no inhibitions. Release all self-criticism and have fun. Tap into the power of your own voice to express and share your inner self with the world.

YOUR TURN FOR SELF-DISCOVERY

Knowing how music affects you is essential in learning how to use music for healing. Mindfulness can help to expand your music listening experience. Observe how each time you listen to a piece of music, the body and mind respond differently.

Self-Inquiry Exercise: Before you begin, find a quiet place and take a few deep breaths to focus your awareness before you start consciously listening to music. In your journal, respond to the following prompts with your thoughts and insights:

- Listen to a piece of music written at around 60 bpm. Refer to the 60 bpm music selections on page 229. Notice and comment on how the body responded before, during, and after your listening experience.

- Listen to a fast-paced workout or dance music selection of your choice. You can easily find music online by searching for music at 120 bpm to 150 bpm. Notice and comment on how the body responded before, during, and after your listening experience.

- Experiment with the five tips in Tune Your Day on page 234. Which of these do you already practice? Which are you willing to add? What did you notice?

- Choose one of the pieces listed next or a selection of your choice and follow the How to Listen suggestions on page 232. Record your imagery experience and how the body, mind, emotions, and soul responded to the music.
  - Wolfgang Amadeus Mozart: Concerto for Flute and Harp, Movement 2
  - Johann Sebastian Bach: Air, Orchestral Suites No. 3 in D Major, Movement 2

- Samuel Barber: Adagio for Strings
- Ludwig van Beethoven: Symphony No. 9, Movement 3
- Claude Debussy: Afternoon of a Faun
- Bill Evans: "Peace Piece"
- Gustav Holst: The Planets, Venus
- Mahalia Jackson: "I Believe"
- Maurice Ravel: Daphnis and Chloe Suite No. 2
- Ottorino Respighi: Pines of Rome: Pines of the Janiculum
- Simon and Garfunkel: "Bridge over Troubled Water"
- Antonio Vivaldi: The Four Seasons, Winter, Movements 1 and 2
- Vaughan Williams: "Fantasia on Greensleeves"

In Closing

Music is a powerful force that has been used in healing for centuries. Many hospitals are acknowledging the benefits of using the energetic designs of sound, music, color, and light in their patient areas to alleviate anxiety, reduce fear and pain, and aid in the healing process. As you have learned, music has many applications. Discover music that inspires and moves you, that touches your heart and soul and expresses your mood and inner feelings. The following are points to remember:

❖ Sound and music preferences differ for people.

❖ When deciding on music for relaxation, choose soft, slow, and calming music that doesn't have sudden loud sounds.

❖ You can use the principle of entrainment to create music as medicine to lower stress and slow the heart and breath rate.

- Creating a music prescription library allows you to have your ideal healing music on hand to help induce the specific moods you desire.

- Tuning in and listening to music consciously can have profound healing effects.

- Use music throughout your day to stay calm, focused, and energized.

I leave you with this thought: Make music a fundamental part of your everyday life. Let music fill you, for as Louis Armstrong says, "Music is life itself."

Congratulations on completing Part Five. If you have been following along, you have learned the following:

- How the human energy field affects health

- What human qualities constitute a low-frequency and high-frequency vibration life

- How to restore and balance your energy to promote wellness

- The principles and value of energy management

- How sound and music can be used as healing tools

Congratulations, you did it!
You have completed this first journey with me.
Thank you.

My Parting Words

This book is centered on the premise that one small change in one area of your life can have a domino effect and create huge changes in all other areas. It's the little changes in caring for ourselves that have the biggest effects and the most impact on our health and wellness. It's about the many little steps along our journey that are filled with discovery and endless possibilities.

To understand wellness, we must understand that we are multidimensional beings that require healing on many levels to achieve health and well-being. Many of us are healing from the effects of stress, which can be contagious. As stress reaches epidemic proportions, we need a proactive and multifaceted approach. Western medicine focuses on a chemical drug approach to reduce stress. However, chronic stress-related illnesses can be helped through complementary and integrative approaches to reduce the negative effects of stress in the body and remove the root cause.

The intention behind this book is to serve as a tool and resource as you face the challenges and overcome the obstacles of everyday life, so you can live a low-stress, elevated life. Each part of this book shared practices, techniques, and self-inquiries to bring you closer to the process of knowing and loving yourself more deeply. Our most valuable relationship is with ourselves.

We all long to feel a sense of wholeness and to live a life filled with love, harmony, and peace. When you access your inner wisdom and align with your true essence and Divine Source, your thoughts, feelings, lifestyle choices, and behaviors support your highest purpose and potential to live in the light. As you follow along your path, old habits and lifestyle patterns may resurface. That's okay. Do not judge yourself. Be aware, observe yourself, and be open to change.

We all have the opportunity to shift our perceptions and create change. We can be present and tap into our own consciousness, where change begins. We can listen, remove the blocks, and nourish the body. We can clear the physical, mental, and emotional clutter that hides our vulnerability, flexibility, and full expression of Self. We can open our hearts and shine our light on the world. We can nurture our souls and expand our awareness to embrace our humanity. We can appreciate our Divine nature and the whole of life.

I wish you well on your continued journey.

Love & Light
Jan

Recommended Reading to Inspire

The Biology of Belief: Unleashing the Power of Consciousness, Matter & Miracles by Bruce H. Lipton, PhD (Tenth anniversary edition; Hay House Inc., 2016)

The Book of Secrets: Unlocking the Hidden Dimensions of Your Life by Deepak Chopra, MD (Harmony Books, 2005)

Change Your Schedule, Change Your Life: How to Harness the Power of Clock Genes to Lose Weight, Optimize Your Workout, and Finally Get a Good Night's Sleep by Suhas Kshirsagar, MD, with Michelle Seaton (Harper Wave, 2019)

Change Your Thoughts—Change Your Life: Living the Wisdom of the Tao by Dr. Wayne W. Dyer (Hay House Publishers India, 2016)

The Dark Side of the Light Chasers: Reclaiming Your Power, Creativity, Brilliance, and Dreams by Debbie Ford (Anniversary edition: Riverhead Books, 2010)

Energy Medicine: Balancing Your Body's Energies for Optimal Health, Joy, and Vitality by Donna Eden with David Feinstein, PhD (First edition; Tarcher-Perigee, 2008)

Healing Anger: The Power of Patience from a Buddhist Perspective by the Dalai Lama (Snow Lion Publishers, New York, 1997)

The Inner Nature of Music and the Experience of Tone by Rudolph Steiner (SteinerBooks, 1983)

Make Anger Your Ally by Neil Clark Warren, PhD (Living Books, 1999)

Perfect Health: The Complete Mind/Body Guide by Deepak Chopra, MD (Harmony Books, 2001)

Siddhartha by Hermann Hesse (Reprint edition; CreateSpace Independent Publishing Platform, 2010)

Stressed Is Desserts Spelled Backward: Rising Above Life's Challenges with Humor, Hope and Courage by Brian Luke Seaward, PhD (Second edition; Whole Person Associates, Inc., 2006)

The Subtle Body: An Encyclopedia of Your Energetic Anatomy by Cyndi Dale (Sounds True, 2009)

The 20-Minute Break: Reduce Stress, Maximize Performance, Improve Health and Emotional Well-Being Using the New Science of Ultradian Rhythms by Ernest Rossi, PhD (Tarcher, 1991)

References

Ariga, A., and A. Lleras. "Brief and Rare Mental 'Breaks' Keep You Focused: Deactivation and Reactivation of Task Goals Preempt Vigilance Decrements." *Cognition* 118, no. 3 (March 2011): 439–43. doi: 10.1016/j.cognition.2010.12.007.

Berbel, P., J. Moix, and S. Quintana. "Music versus Diazepam to Reduce Preoperative Anxiety: A Randomized Controlled Clinical Trial." *Revista Española de Anestesiología y Reanimación* 54, no. 6 (June 2007): 355–58. www.ncbi.nlm.nih.gov/pubmed/17695946.

Capacchione, Lucia, PhD. *The Creative Journal: The Art of Finding Yourself.* Wayne, NJ: Career Press, 2001.

Chanda, Mona Lisa, and Daniel J. Levitin. "The Neurochemistry of Music." *Trends in Cognitive Sciences* 17, no. 4 (April 2013): 179–93. https://doi.org/10.1016/j.tics.2013.02.007.

Davis, William, PhD, Kate Gfeller, PhD, and Michael H. Thaut, PhD. *An Introduction to Music Therapy: Theory and Practice.* 3rd ed. Silver Spring, MD: The American Music Therapy Association, 2008.

de Almondes, K. M., M. V. Costa, L. F. Malloy-Diniz, and B. S. Diniz. "Insomnia and Risk of Dementia in Older Adults: Systematic Review and Meta-Analysis." *Journal of Psychiatric Research* 77 (June 2016): 109–15. doi: 10.1016/j.jpsychires.2016.02.021.

Deshmukh, Abhijeet D., Avani A. Sarvaiya, Seethalakshmi Ramanathan, and Ajita S. Nayak. "Effect of Indian Classical Music on Quality of Sleep in Depressed Patients: A Randomized Controlled Trial." *Nordic Journal of Music Therapy* 18, no. 1 (2009): 70–78. doi: 10.1080/08098130802697269.

Ferreri, Laura, Ernest Mas-Herrero, Robert J. Zatorre, Pablo Ripollés, Alba Gomez-Andres, Helena Alicart, Guillem Olivé, et al. "Dopamine Modulates the Reward Experiences Elicited by Music." *Proceedings of the National Academy of Sciences* 116, no. 9 (February 2019): 3793–98. www.pnas.org/content/116/9/3793.

Frawley, David, Dr. "What Is Your Real Identity? Going Beyond All Outer Identity to Universal Awareness." American Institute of Vedic Studies. March 28, 2018. Accessed October 8, 2019. www.vedanet.com/what-is-your-real-identity-going-beyond-all-outer-identity-to-universal-awareness/.

Gaynor, Mitchell L, MD. *The Healing Power of Sound: Recovery from Life-Threatening Illness Using Sound, Voice and Music.* 1st ed. Boulder, CO: Shambhala Publications, 2002.

Gaynor, Mitchell L, MD. *Sounds of Healing: A Physician Reveals the Therapeutic Power of Sound, Voice, and Music.* 1st ed. New York, NY: Broadway Books, 1999.

Gerber, Richard, MD. *Vibrational Medicine: The #1 Handbook of Subtle-Energy Therapies.* New York, NY: William Morrow Paperbacks, 2001.

Grape, C., M. Sandgren, L. O. Hansson, M. Ericson, and T. Theorell. "Does Singing Promote Well-Being?: An Empirical Study of Professional and Amateur Singers During a Singing Lesson." *Integrative Psychological and Behavioral Science* 38, no. 1 (January 2002): 65–74. doi: 10.1007/BF02734261.

Keyes, Laurel Elizabeth. *Toning: The Creative Power of the Voice.* 1st ed. Camarillo, CA: DeVorss & Company, 1973.

Krystal, Andrew D., MD, MS. "Psychiatric Disorders and Sleep." *Neurologic Clinics* 30, no. 4 (November 2012): 1389–1413. doi: 10.1016/j.ncl.2012.08.018.

Maman, Fabien, and Terres Unsoeld. *The Tao of Sound: Acoustic Sound Healing for the 21st Century.* Malibu, CA: Tama-Do, The Academy of Sound, Color and Movement, 2008.

National Sleep Foundation. "2014 Sleep in America Poll: Sleep in the Modern Family: Summary of Findings." PDF file. Accessed October 8, 2019. www.sleepfoundation.org/sites/default/files/inline-files/2014-NSF-Sleep-in-America-poll-summary-of-findings—FINAL-Updated-3-26-14-.pdf.

National Wellness Institute. "About Wellness." Accessed October 8, 2019. www.nationalwellness.org/page/AboutWellness.

Rossi, Ernest Lawrence, PhD. *The 20-Minute Break: Reduce Stress, Maximize Performance, Improve Health and Emotional Well-Being Using the New Science of Ultradian Rhythms.* New York, NY: Tarcher, 1991.

Salimpoor, Valorie N., Mitchel Benovoy, Kevin Larcher, Alain Dagher, and Robert J. Zatorre. "Anatomically Distinct Dopamine Release During Anticipation and Experience of Peak Emotion to Music." *Nature Neuroscience* 14, no. 2 (February 2011): 257–62. doi: 10.1038/nn.2726.

Schmidt, Norman B., J. Anthony Richey, Michael J. Zvolensky, and Jon K. Maner. "Exploring Human Freeze Responses to a Threat Stressor." *Journal of Behavior Therapy and Experimental Psychiatry* 39, no. 3 (September 2008): 292–304. doi: 10.1016/j.jbtep.2007.08.002.

Shi, L., S. J. Chen, M. Y. Ma, Y. P. Bao, Y. Han, Y. M. Wang, J. Shi, M. V. Vitiello, and L. Lu. "Sleep Disturbances Increase the Risk of Dementia: A Systematic Review and Meta-Analysis." *Sleep Medicine Reviews* 40 (August 2017): 4–16. doi: 10.1016/j.smrv.2017.06.010.

Shree Chitrabhanu, Gurudev. *The Psychology of Enlightenment: Meditations on the Seven Energy Centers.* New York, NY: Dodd, Mead and Co., 1979.

Stuckey, Heather L., and Jeremy Nobel, MD, MPH. "The Connection Between Art, Healing, and Public Health: A Review of Current Literature." *American Journal of Public Health* 100, no. 2 (February 2010): 254–263. doi: 10.2105/AJPH.2008.156497.

Thoma, Myriam V., Roberto La Marca, Rebecca Brönnimann, Linda Finkel, Ulrike Ehlert, and Urs M. Nater. "The Effect of Music on the Human Stress Response. *PLoS One* 8, no. 8 (2013): e70156. doi: 10.1371/journal.pone.0070156.

Watts, Alan. "Hermits in NY." Awakin.org. Accessed October 8, 2019. www.awakin.org/read/view.php?tid=264.

Acknowledgments

Setting out to write a book has been both challenging and rewarding. From the depths of my heart, I extend my deepest gratitude and express my love to those who have inspired, loved, and supported me to follow my path and share my journey in this book.

To Dr. Ford Kinder (aka Clifford Kinder), my best friend, husband, and loving angel. Thank you for being my biggest supporter, encouraging me for over four decades to never let go of my vision and, for years, urging me to write this book. It has been a great comfort knowing you are always there to lift me up.

To my mother, Jean Siudmak, for continuing to be my guiding light and for teaching me unconditional love, compassion, and determination.

To my father, Dr. John Siudmak, for showing me self-discipline and for the wonderful and divine gift of music you gave me.

To my amazing editor, Carol Killman Rosenberg, for sharing your incredible expertise, for your patience when I said I would have the manuscript to you in a week and two months passed, and for putting me at ease during the writing of this book.

To Gary Rosenberg, book designer, for reading my mind and creating the most wonderful cover design and layout.

To Brian Luke Seaward, PhD, for your friendship, sense of humor, and heartfelt guidance, which continue to inspire me. I am extremely grateful for your kind contribution in the Foreword to this book.

To my principal mentors for your invaluable knowledge, support, and inspiration that will be forever cherished: Dr. Deepak Chopra, Dr. David Simon, Brian Luke Seaward, PhD, Roger Gabriel, Fabien Maman, Terres Unsoeld, and Julianne Bien. Thank you.

To Tina Pugliese for your enthusiasm and gracious support in helping publicize my book.

To Eileen Tanne for your unwavering support, honest feedback, and book-promotion efforts.

To all my patients, clients, and students I've had the honor of working together with for sharing your innermost lives with me and inspiring me to look deeper within myself.

To all the children and students (you know who you are) for sharing your creative selves, letting me see life through your eyes, and keeping me young at heart.

To my colleagues for your friendship, dedication, and courage in helping to create my vision for The Self Centre International in St. John: Brian Young, Judy Heaney, Elizabeth Escardo, Dr. M. Kelley Hunter, Eric Lalich, Irene Levin, Oriel Smith, Elizabeth Gowan, Jude Woodcock, Lawrence Ford, Ronni Ford, Lurane Worth, Rosanne Perkins, Ruth Ann David, Emily Sorenson, Carla Murray, Lori Doherty Francis, Vicky Pedersen, Giuliana Cassataro, Ofer Elyakim, Peggy Blitz, Brion Morrisette, and Jennifer Hawkins and Kristin Hutton Moller of Hawkins International Public Relations.

To my early supporters and friends for sharing your expertise with me and for helping me bring my visions to fruition: Dr. Catherine Campbell; Dr. Howard Rusk; Dr. Jeanne Bresciani; Richard Buckingham

Clarke; Ruth "Sis" Frank; Rudy Wells; Elroy Sprauve; Faye Fredericks; Kim Wild; Martin Nicholson; Barbara Nicholson; Vicki Bell; Karen Samuel; Jim Provost; Terri Provost; the faculty, parents, students, and supporters of St. John School of the Arts; and colleagues Marie Shanahan, Dr. Brent Forward, Barbara D'Alessio, and Dr. Ken Harris.

To Talib Schwartz for being a remarkable healer and helping me through the autoimmune situation and being on-call for me no matter what time of day or night.

To my loving family, who have been an integral part of my journey: my brothers, Dr. Bob Siudmak, Bill Siudmak, and Don Siudmak, for always being there for me; my cousin, Michelle Dussault, for our sisterly bond and being my confidant; my brothers-in-law, Max Geiger and Jeff Kinder, for sharing your talents and supporting my venture; and my sweet healing dog, Asia, for shining your beautiful light on my clients.

To my lifelong friends, Bette Mercedes and Lorraine Seidel, for your unshakable love and honesty and for standing by me through thick and thin.

To Craig Dengler for the many hours you spent listening to me brainstorm or babble and then sharing your creative input.

To Julienne Bien for your encouragement and knowing I could count on you to bounce off ideas and get a clear perspective.

To all my old and new friends and colleagues for your enthusiastic encouragement. To anyone I have not named specifically, please know that I value your contribution to my life.

And last, but most important, I want to thank God for creating me and giving me the power to manifest my soul's desires. I am eternally grateful.

About the Author

Jan Kinder, RN, is a leader in wellness and a pioneer in holistic nursing and the healing arts. She dedicates her career to teach, guide, and support adults and youth in promoting self-awareness, self-care, and self-discovery as avenues for healing and health, harmony and balance, and to embrace all aspects of well-being. She is a registered nurse with a BA in psychology and a music therapist. She holds board certifications in both holistic nursing and health and wellness nurse coaching and was among the first Chopra Center certified instructors. For more than thirty-five years, she has blended her credentialed expertise in integrative wellness practices, stress management, meditation, music and the creative and expressive therapies, vibrational sound and color healing, energy therapies, guided imagery, Ayurveda, and neuro-linguistic programming (NLP).

She is founder of the Jan Kinder Center for Health and Well-Being, LLC, in South Florida (2012), originally the Mind Body Health Institute in New Jersey (1996), and formerly The Self Centre International, LLC (2000), the award-winning and innovative mind-body-spirit wellness center at the prestigious Caneel Bay Resort in St. John, USVI, where she was featured in such publications as *Organic Spa*, *Wall Street Journal*, *Travel and Leisure*, *LA Confidential*, and *Palm Beach Illustrated*. Dr. Deepak Chopra, author of *How to Know God*, says, "Jan Kinder has dedicated herself to heal, to love, to transform and to serve others. She is an inspiration to those around her."

As an international speaker, participants consider Jan to be a "motivating, funny, and warmhearted presenter with integrity, compassion, and many gifts and talents." Over the years, she has served various populations in hospital/medical organizations, major corporations, universities, schools, yoga and meditation centers, and the private sector. Her background also includes program development and implementation for multicultural and community-outreach programs, and services to special needs and underserved and at-risk youth.

Among her lifelong endeavors, Jan is an accomplished classical pianist, composer, and former TV "jingle" singer. She is a contributing author in the bestselling book *Conversations That Make a Difference: Stories Supporting a Bigger Vision.* She divides her professional career between her private practice in Delray Beach, Florida, offering virtual and in-person sessions, workshops, retreats, and speaking engagements.

The theme in her lifelong work encompasses the mind-body-spirit interrelatedness and focuses on the quality of life.

Contact Information

To schedule a session with Jan Kinder or to arrange to have her speak at your event, contact her at Jan@JanKinder.com. You can also visit Jan's website at www.JanKinder.com.

www.ingramcontent.com/pod-product-compliance
Lightning Source LLC
Chambersburg PA
CBHW051353290426
44108CB00015B/1993